ALEXANDER

MILITARY PROFILES
SERIES EDITOR
Dennis E. Showalter, Ph.D.
Colorado College

*Instructive summaries for general and expert
readers alike, volumes in the Military Profiles
series are essential treatments of significant and
popular military figures drawn from world history,
ancient times through the present.*

ALEXANDER

Invincible King of Macedonia

Peter G. Tsouras

BRASSEY'S, INC.
Washington, D.C.

Library of Congress Cataloging-in-Publication Data
Tsouras, Peter.
Alexander: invincible king of Macedonia / Peter G Tsouras.
p. cm.— (Military profiles)
Includes bibliographical references and index.
ISBN 1-57488-407-7 — ISBN 1-57488-697-5
1. Alexander, the Great, 356-323 B.C.—Military leadership. I. Title.
II. Series.
DF234.2.T73   2003
355'.0092—dc21   2003007788

Hardcover ISBN 1-57488-407-7
Softcover ISBN 1-57488-697-5
(alk. paper)

Printed in the United States of America on acid-free paper that meets the American National Standards Institute z39-48 Standard.

Brassey's, Inc.
22841 Quicksilver Drive
Dulles, Virginia 20166

FIRST EDITION

10 9 8 7 6 5 4 3 2 1

To my grandmothers, the gentle maids from Knossos and Arcadian Orchomenos, who gave me Homer and poetry.

Contents

Maps

Preface

"I sing of warfare and a man of war."[1] This opening line of Virgil's *Aeneid* describes the Trojan hero, Aeneas, progenitor of Rome, but Aeneas is only the faint outline of what underneath is the true heroic and martial ideal—Alexander the Great. The Macedonian was then and remains the touchstone by which those who embrace the profession of arms measure all things. Julius Caesar wept when he realized that at an age when Alexander had made himself master of so many kings, he had accomplished nothing. Chandragupta, the first unifier of India, may have seen Alexander in person and was inspired by the spark of example to build an empire.

Above all, Alexander was "a man of war." It is Alexander as leader, soldier, and general that this book will explore. War clings to his name in both history and legend. He became the unattainable standard for which Roman emperors, medieval kings, and steppe barbarians thirsted. Even to this day, as these lines are penned, a city he named for himself, modern Kandahar in Afghanistan, rattles again with the noise of war.

Genius is a word that leaps to embrace Alexander. Clausewitz said genius was the realm "which rises above all rules."[2] He caught the underlying truth of Alexander who relentlessly triumphed against the impossible. Appian compared him to "a brilliant flash of lightning" that so shook his world, we still see the reflected brightness. Napoleon, who had a good share of this fire as well, made it clear that such triumph is not a spur-of-the-moment thing or luck but is based on planning and good judgment. If Alexander always seemed blessed by luck, it was because chance always favors the prepared mind. The image of Alexander as hero obscures his deep intellect, the kingdom of the strategist and logistician where shrewd good judgment and patience trump heroics. He could not have subdued Greece, destroyed the Persian Empire, and rampaged down the Indus had he not planned and weighed his moves carefully. Yet when time came for action, he wasted no time. The tempo and speed of his operations were always running over the decision cycles of his enemy.

Strategy and logistics brought him advantageously to battle where the tactician and leader of men came to the fore. He fought no two battles the same. J. F. C. Fuller noted, "The military genius is he who can produce original combinations out of the forces of war; he is the man who can take all these forces and so attune them to the conditions which confront him that he can produce startling and, frequently, incomprehensible results."[3] In each of his battles, Alexander immediately imposed his will upon his enemies by seizing the initiative in a stunning way. The reader can sense the utter bewilderment of his enemies as events overwhelmed them. They were undone by his mind as much as by the Macedonian army.

That army was another element of his genius, attached to him by an emotional umbilical as few armies have ever been. "An army which had Alexander . . . under its eye was different from itself in its simple nature, it imbibed a share of [his] divine spirit, became insensible of danger, and heroic in the extreme."[4] It was the supreme example of the exaltation of men engaged in great and heroic enterprises. As he said, "[H]ardship and danger are the price of glory, and that sweet is the savour of a life of courage and of deathless renown beyond the grave." In essence, Alexander and the Macedonian army were lovers (*philos* not *eros*) with all the demands and proofs of love. One day he would remind them that he bore no wound upon his back and that none of them had died in battle from wounds in the back. This shared heroic ideal was the heart of the bond. He would never ask them to do what he would not, and they would do everything he asked. Everything rested on this bond; Alexander was great as long as he remained faithful to it.

Above all, Alexander believed in himself. As a child he had been imbued with a sense of the heroic ideal straight out of the *Iliad* as the ultimate in human existence—to be the best in battle and in virtue. He lived this ideal intensely, and when he failed it, his sanity almost fled. In Alexander the heroic ideal received a new dimension through philosophy and the study of man. His chivalry toward enemies and especially women startled a brutal world. The hard-hearted Hellenes thought it an eccentricity but internalized it and passed it on to later ages as an ideal. But the heroic ideal was a human one, and when he became obsessed with godhood, he let go of the ideal.

His path to glory was flooded with blood, an accepted fact of life to the ancients despite the distress it causes to moderns. That he could have spilled far more in that context and did not speaks to the man. He was seldom cruel. What astounded the ancients was not the blood and the cruelty but that he publicly regretted them.

There have been other great captains who are mentioned in the same breath—Caesar, Genghis Khan, Napoleon—but none mastered every aspect of war with such success and such a perfection as did Alexander. He did this all before he had reached thirty-three years of age and died at the height of his success. Even in this he surpassed all his rivals for he passed into legend before the fateful bargain with divinity took its due.

No book is ever done alone, and I offer my heartfelt thanks to those who helped and encouraged me. To Ralph Peters who urged me on when I was in the worst writer's block of my life; to my wife, Patty, who always supports me and creates the maps as well; to Jona Lendering who graciously offered me photos from his collection; to my editor, Paul Merzlak who smoothed all the problems; to my agent, Fritz Heinzen, for his golden advice; and above all to Alexander. It was on his birthday that my writer's block collapsed in a flood of energy.

Peter G. Tsouras
Alexandria, Virginia
Winter 2002

Chronology

333   Story of the Gordian Knot. Suffers severe illness, *August.* Mounts Battle of Issus, *October/November.* Refuses Darius' first peace offer.

332   Submission of Phoenicia, *January.* Persian fleet breaks up, *Spring.* Siege of Tyre, *January–July.* Refuses Darius' second peace offer, *June.* Siege of Gaza, *September–October.* Crowned pharaoh in Memphis, *November.*

331   Visit to shrine of Ammon-Ra, *early Spring.* Founds Alexandria, *April.* Crosses Euphrates, *August.* Crosses Tigris, *September 18.* Battle of Gaugamela, *October 1.* Babylon falls, *late October.* Occupies Susa, *December.*

330   Forces Persian Gates and sacks Persepolis, *January.* Burns palace at Persepolis, *May.* Pursues Darius, *June.* Darius murdered, *July.* Marches to Drangiana, *August.* Conspiracy of Philotas and murder of Parmenion, *October.* Marches through Arachosia.

329   Crosses Hindu Kush, *March–April.* Occupies Batricia, *April–May.* Pursues Bessus across Oxus, *June.* Bessus surrenders. Revolt of Spitamenes, *Fall.* Defeats Scythians, *Fall.*

328   Campaign against Spitamenes. Murder of Cleitus, *August.*

327   Defeats Spitamenes. Captures Sogdian Rock, *late Winter.* Pages Conspiracy, *Spring.* Marries Roxane.

326   Invades India. Crosses Indus, *April.* Battle of the Hydaspes and Bucephalus dies, *May.* Mutiny on the Hyphasis, *July.* Fleet moves downriver, *November.* Alexander badly wounded in campaign against the Mallians, *November–December.*

325   Reaches Patala and builds fleet, *July.* Crosses Gedrosian Desert, *September.* Purges corrupt satraps, *December.* Fleet arrives and Craterus arrives with the rest of the army, *December.*

ALEXANDER

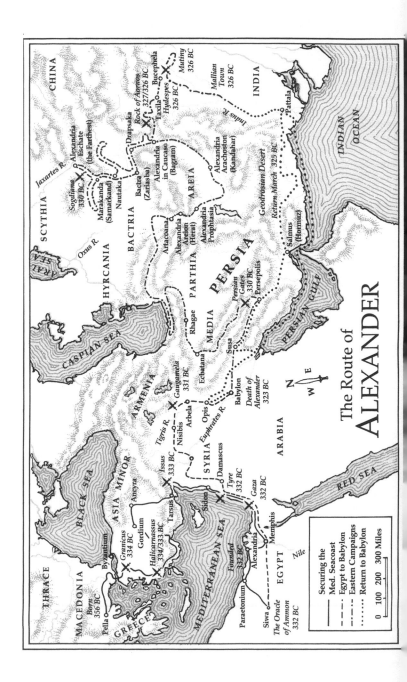

The Route of ALEXANDER

CHINA

Mutiny 326 BC

INDIA

Mallian Town 326 BC

Alexandria Eschate (the Farthest)

Rock of Aornos 327/326 BC

Bucephala

Taxila

Hydaspes 326 BC

Drapsaka

Jaxartes R.

Sogdiana 330 BC

Marakanda (Samarkand)

Nautaka

Bactra (Zariasa)

Alexandria in Caucaso (Bagram)

Alexandria Arachoston (Kandahar)

SCYTHIA

Oxus R.

BACTRIA

AREIA

Indus R.

Pattala

INDIAN OCEAN

ARAL SEA

HYRCANIA

Artacoana

Alexandria Areion (Herat)

Alexandria Prophtasia

Gedrosian Desert

Return March 325 BC

Salmus (Hormuz)

CASPIAN SEA

PARTHIA

PERSIA

Rhagae

Persian Gates

Persepolis

PERSIAN GULF

ARMENIA

MEDIA

Ecbatana

Susa

Gaugamela 331 BC

Tigris R.

Nisibis

Arbela

Opis

Babylon Death of Alexander 323 BC

Euphrates R.

N
W E

Rhagae

THRACE

MACEDONIA

Born 356 BC

Pella

GREECE

Byzantium

BLACK SEA

ASIA MINOR

Ancyra

Gordium

Granicus 334 BC

Halicarnassus 334/333 BC

Tarsus

Issus 333 BC

SYRIA

Damascus

Sidon

Tyre 332 BC

Gaza 332 BC

Memphis

Founded 332 BC

Alexandria

Paraetonium

Siwa

The Oracle of Ammon 332 BC

EGYPT

Nile

MEDITERRANEAN SEA

RED SEA

ARABIA

Securing the
Med. Seacoast
Egypt to Babylon
Eastern Campaigns
Return to Babylon

0 100 200 300 Miles

Chapter 1

Philip

ALEXANDER III was born on 20 July 356 B.C., as heir of the Argead dynasty of the Kingdom of Macedonia in northeastern Greece. His father, Philip II, was probably the most remarkable Greek military and political figure between Pericles and Alexander himself. If Alexander's accomplishments shine so brightly, it is because he stood upon the shoulders of a giant. Philip transformed Macedonia from a minor and constantly beleaguered state into the mistress of Hellas and created the magnificent weapon of war—the Macedonian army.

Macedonia means "Land of the Tall," a good description for the hardy nation of farmers, herdsmen, and independent nobility. The Macedonians were Greek in language and blood but did not share the city-state culture of the southern Greeks who were quick to lump their cruder kinsmen with barbarians. That their dialect was unintelligible in the south encouraged that attitude. Macedonia resembled more the vanished world described in Homer's *Iliad* where the nobility lived hard, drank hard, and fought hard. Through this "Heroic" world, however, Greek culture and arts had permeated. Alexander's royal ancestors hosted the artistic genius of Greece, and the nobility slowly came to accept a Greek education and eventually picked up the language as well. Euripides composed his masterpiece, The *Bacchae*, in Pella as a guest at the Macedonion court. The Macedonians had a finer taste for the arts of war.

These arts had been finely honed for more than a hundred years beginning with the Peloponnesian Wars in which Athens and Sparta contested for the mastery of Greece. With Athens' fall, Sparta held sway, only to be humbled in turn by Thebes. Into Thebes at its moment of supremacy, young Philip was sent as a hostage (369–365 B.C.) by his elder brother Peridiccas III as recognition of that hegemony which extended even into Macedonia. The Thebans, to their ultimate regret, provided a superb military education to the man who would transform Macedonia from a minor backwater to the dominant power in Greece and whose son would obliterate their city. Shortly before Philip's arrival, the great Theban general, Epaminondas had won the decisive victory at Leuctra (371 B.C.) that had permanently broken Spartan power. Innovative tactics that refused, or pulled back, one flank and weighted the other into an irresistible fist had smashed the traditional Spartan phalanx and left the Spartans dead in heaps, destroying their ancient legend of invincibility.

Philip learned two great military lessons in Thebes: (1) the necessity for tactical flexibility, and (2) the critical importance of combined arms, which had played little role in the phalanx system. The phalanx was essentially the city's citizen levy, all the men who could afford the panoply of a hoplite, a heavily armed spearman who fought in a disciplined formation usually eight men deep. Encased in bronze armor, with a large, round, bronze shield and an eight-foot spear, the hoplites made the phalanx the supreme fighting machine of Greece. The hoplite was invincible against the poor infantry of Asia, but against other Greeks the phalanx was an inflexible formation incapable of serious maneuver. All that was expected of it was to meet a similar force in a savage stabbing and shoving match, the "push of pike."

Other arms were coming into importance to strengthen the

phalanx. Long periods of war bred mercenaries who were often light troops able to skirmish effectively and outmarch the unwieldy phalanx. The great mercenary general, Iphicrates, had completely recast the light infantry into a formidable force by giving them a light and flexible body armor of pleated linen and a small shield. To offset the lighter protection, he provided a longer spear to outreach the better-defended hoplite. Thus in addition to the advantage of mobility derived from the lighter equipment, the light infantryman's longer spear had the offensive reach on the hoplite. Cavalry, however, had remained as little more than flank guards and reconnaissance because of the prohibitive cost of raising warhorses on the extremely limited agricultural land. Continual campaigning by the Greeks on the periphery of Macedonia, Thessaly, and Thrace had given them many opportunities to see cavalry as a potential offensive arm. For the hostage Philip, the potential was exploitable. Macedonia was ideal horse country, rich in broad, well-watered pastures and fields.

With this education fresh in hand, the young Philip was called home by the disaster of 359 B.C. in which Perdiccas and four thousand Macedonians were killed in an Illyrian invasion. His arrival probably saved Macedonia from extinction at the hands of powerful neighbors. He was appointed regent for Perdiccas' infant son but so quickly proved his worth that he was acclaimed king by the army and the child was set aside. Philip quickly demonstrated a talent for organization and good government. He was a just man, secure enough to admit to the mistake, a fact the folk memories captured. On one occasion, he brushed aside an old woman among others who were trying to present him petitions. The old woman was particularly insistent, and he curtly told her he was too busy. She retorted, "Then give up being king." Taken aback at her rebuke and acknowledging his failure, he heard her petition on the spot and the others' as well.[1]

Philip found no real army in Macedonia. Rather, he had a body of heavy cavalry comprising the nobility of the kingdom who owed service to the king and were named his Companions or the Companion Cavalry. The name is indicative of the social relationship. Macedonian kings were not the absolute or divine rulers of Asia but Indo-European chieftains writ large, *primus inter pares* rather than *rex*. The nobility did not unduly strain their necks by looking up to their kings at too sharp an angle. For them it was only slightly off the horizontal. They fully expected to speak their minds and rarely hesitated to do so. The infantry was only feudal levies indifferently armed and trained.

Philip's solution was to create a standing army, the first in Europe. He paid for it by conquering lucrative gold mines whose income supported a year-round force. He expanded and regularized the Companion Cavalry, dividing them into permanent squadrons. He also added another eight hundred men. He took a more decisive step when he established a permanent and disciplined infantry element—the Foot Companions to parallel the Companion Cavalry. The importance of these two steps should not be underestimated. By increasing the part of the male population devoted to this new permanent army, he vastly increased the proportion of the population that had a stake both in the military success of the kingdom and in the survival and prosperity of Philip and his dynasty. From military service came many of rewards—titles, land, and office for the Companion Cavalry and regular and steady pay for the Foot Companions and the opportunity to rise by ability. For both groups, there was also the opportunity for loot, not to mention the heady attraction of an adventurous and glorious life.

Philip strengthened the cohesion of the kingdom more than with just the opportunity for material advancement. Traditionally, the assembly of the army, which had meant essentially the small circle of the Companion Cavalry, had the right to acclaim its choice as king from the ruling dynasty. It had also anticipated King John's knights at Runnymede by requiring any capital crime carrying the death penalty to be tried before the army as judge and jury. Now these rights were extended from the nobility to the enlarged army. The personal relationship between army and ruler had become elements of strength and unity. Philip's genius was to respect the institution of the army assembly without allowing it to ever really limit or oppose anything he chose to do.

Among Philip's virtues was the ability to attract and retain the services of other talented men such as the exceptional generals, Parmenion and Antipater. Once after having slept a long time on campaign, Philip remarked, "I slept soundly because Antipater was awake."[2] On another occasion, he remarked that he thought the Athenians were extremely lucky because every year they elected ten generals. He, on the other hand, had been able to find only one—Parmenion. Philip was forever binding men to him, whether through an extensive system of guest friendships with the most notable men of Greece or with the humble men about him. Philip was warned that one of his best soldiers, Pythias, had become hostile because in his poverty he could not support his three daughters, and the king had not offered to help. Philip replied, "What! If part of my body were diseased, should I cut it off rather than give it treatment?" He then spoke to Pythias privately, provided help, and thereby earned an even more devoted follower.[3]

The new Foot Companions he now grouped into phalanx regiments of about fifteen hundred men raised by canton. Instead of the heavy bronze panoply and shield of the hoplite, he built upon the innovations of Iphicrates and introduced new elements. For their offensive arm, he gave his fighters a fifteen-foot pike, or sarissa, that easily outreached the hoplite's eight-foot spear. He also equipped them with a stout helmet and linen or leather body armor and metal greaves for the lower legs. So that the heavy sarissa could be grasped with both hands to give it greater thrust and control than the hoplite spear, he affixed a small round shield to the upper left arm. The traditional phalanx had been a single mass of infantry that could not be maneuvered once it had been set in motion. Philip's reorganization changed that. Each regiment could maneuver independently and quickly. When moving to contact, the overall phalanx did not charge but moved steadily and inexorably forward. Its depth was eventually fixed at sixteen men. The first five ranks would advance with leveled sarissas presenting a powerfully thrusting hedge of steel, while the remaining ranks were held front to rear in a rising arc which served to deflect descending arrows, javelins, and sling stones. It was a vast improvement over anything the city-states of the south could put into the field.

The only vulnerability was to a flank attack. To solve this problem and to add the necessary flexibility to this phalanx-cavalry combination, Philip created another formation, the Hypaspists or Guards, equipped like the Macedonian phalangist but armed with a larger shield and a spear. The Guards were trained for the most flexible of operations, protecting the flank of the phalanx and maintaining contact between the phalanx and the cavalry. They also engaged in what would today be called special operations.

To his Macedonian formations, Philip added the best of the fighting men from the regions he subdued. Particularly important were the Thessalian cavalry, every bit as good as the Companion Cavalry. These entered Philip's army when he became archon of Thessaly. Thracians and Agrianes supplied superb light infantry. Philip also made extensive use of Greek talent. Not only did he hire large numbers of their well-trained infantry mercenaries, but he also used them as artillerymen and engineers. Many Greeks of proven ability who had settled in Macedonia were also enrolled in his Companion Cavalry.

Another of Philip's innovations was the creation of the world's first artillery train made up of the newly developed torsion catapults. This also included a siege train. Not the least of his innovations was a permanent supply train, a vast improvement over the ad hoc Greek practice.

For Philip, the Companion Cavalry was his hammer, and the phalanx his anvil. The phalanx would fix, or hold in place, the enemy infantry while the cavalry would provide the offensive shock element that would strike flank or rear, the most vulnerable parts of the traditional Greek phalanx. The Guards would provide the flexible hinges that kept the army an articulated whole rather than disjointed and vulnerable fragments in the heat of battle. In the operational use of this deadly new instrument, Philip went far beyond his Greek teachers in the art of war—to them, victory meant driving the enemy off the field of battle and possessing it. Philip cut to the core of war. For him, destruction of the enemy was the paramount determination of victory. And for this, the cavalry was the necessary arm to engage in a ruthless pursuit of the enemy until his army was broken beyond repair. Philip could have coined the axioms, "Always press hard on the heels of a rout" and "The fruits of victory are gathered in the pursuit." It was a lesson in which the son would spectacularly outshine the father.

Philip also demonstrated a profound understanding of the ebb and flow of opportunity. He was the ultimate pragmatist who would have scoffed at risking a battle over a point of honor. He could patiently wait for his moment in the complex interplay of diplomacy, espionage, and war. He was to say, "I do not flee, but I give ground like the rams, in order that I might make my charge the mightier."[4] Demosthenes, the brilliant Athenian statesman and politician and Philip's most unrelenting and bitter foe, summed up his advance across Greece in several magnificent but ultimately useless speeches to the people of Athens. From him we get the synonym for an *ad hominum* tirade—the Phillippic. "No wonder that Philip, sharing himself in the toils of the campaign, present at every action, neglecting no chance and wasting no season, gets the better of us, while we procrastinate and pass resolutions and ask questions."[5] Greek politicians were in a constant state of surprise at Philip's incomparable talents in the more shadowy spectrum of war—deception, intrigue, and bribery. Told once that a fort he wanted to take was impenetrable, "he asked if it were so difficult that not even an ass laden with money could approach it."[6] There was one more talent, one that perplexed and demoralized enemies. Philip was charmingly lethal at personally disarming them. Demosthenes railed at Philip's ability to manipulate men, at his charismatic hold on so many of leading men who would betray their own cities for the sake of his "friendship."

The Athenian politicians, luckier than they knew, spewed a constant stream of venom at Philip over decades, always imagining he wanted to sack their fair city. Carrying fire and sword to Athens was the last thing on his mind. He held the city as the light of Hellas, accorded its achievements the greatest respect, and inwardly sought its approval in his mission to unify Greece. He only wanted to humble it politically. For its politicians, and he must have had Demosthenes much in mind, he said that they made him a better man, "since I try to prove by word and deed that they are liars." In a more pungent comment, he said that the Athenians were like busts of the god Hermes—all mouth and dick.[7]

Many years later in Asia, Alexander himself would remind his Macedonians of the transformation Philip had wrought.

> Philip found you a tribe of impoverished vagabonds, most of you dressed in skins, feeding a few sheep on the hills and fighting, feebly enough, to keep them from your neighbors . . . he taught you to fight on equal terms with the enemy on our borders, till you knew that your safety lay not, as once, in your mountains strongholds, but in your own valour. . . . [A]nd when he was made supreme commander of all the rest of Greece for the war against Persia, he claimed the glory not for himself alone, but for the Macedonian people.[8]

Philip, above all, was the rare creative genius in history, a profound innovator who gleaned every lesson he could from the Greeks but then went far beyond them in the creation of the first truly modern army. J. R. Hamilton captures the achievement, "Not only did constant training and campaigning forge the disparate elements into a military machine unmatched in Greek warfare but its almost unbroken success must have materially assisted in creating a feeling of unity and patriotism in Macedonia. The army was Philip's greatest legacy to his son."[9]

The Greeks who had borne the brunt of it best expressed the dread of Macedonian fury. One of the Companions speaks for himself in a fragment of an anti-Macedonian play, *Philip*, by Mnesicmachus.

Have you any idea
What we're like to fight against? Our sort make their dinner
Off honed-up swords, and swallow blazing torches
For a savoury snack. Then, by way of dessert,
They bring us, not nuts, but broken arrow-heads
And splintered spear shafts. For pillows we make do
With our shields and breastplates; arrows and slings lie strewn
Under our feet, and we wreathe our brows with catapults.[10]

Philip left Alexander not only a powerful state and army, but more important, he served as priceless example and teacher of generalship, statecraft, diplomacy, and the art of leading men. He bequeathed to Alexander a relentlessness of purpose and a flexibility of method that uniformly yielded success. Alexander had the priceless fortune to be schooled in the arts of kingship and war by a man who was a master of both.

Chapter 2

The Eaglet

Aᴌᴇxᴀɴᴅᴇʀ ᴡᴀs ʙᴏʀɴ on 20 July 356 B.C., under the sign of Leo, the Lion. Philip named him Alexander. It was a royal name of the dynasty, and the child would someday be Alexander III. It was a kingly name, meaning Protector of Men. Almost immediately the legends began to grow about the rush of victories that accompanied his birth—Parmenion's victory over the Illyrians and the victory of his father's chariot in the race at the Olympic games. How much they were after-the-fact additions is unknown, but what was important was that it was a believing age in which divine favor was a given.

The aura of victory would have meant little had Alexander's parents not given him a superlative genetic advantage. They were two of the most able people of their age. From both he inherited iron will. Philip's talents we have already seen. Alexander's mother was his match and his complement, adding fire and passion to Philip's strategy and calculation.

She was Olympias, daughter of the late Epirot king Neoptolemus. Philip was a youth, the younger son of a king, when he saw her at the initiation ceremonies into the religious mysteries of Samothrace. The story was that he fell madly in love with her. It was easy to see why he had been smitten. Younger than he, her beauty was already apparent and intoxicating. She was not the typical Greek woman whose glory was never to be spoken of. Red-haired and fiery by nature, she was a woman for whom power was an all-consuming pursuit. To Philip she was not only an object of initial passion but of political utility; he was a king two years when he married her in 357 B.C. By marrying into the Epirot royal family, he secured the southwestern flank of Macedonia. He strengthened that link by later placing Olympias' brother, Alexander, on the throne of Epirus in 342 B.C. In Alexander, Olympias secured her place as queen mother by providing Philip with an heir. Without Alexander she would never have been more than a secondary wife and diplomatic pawn. Understandably, she invested in him all her hopes and fears.

Those fears were to become more and more animated by Philip's wandering eye for both sexes. That proclivity was given a push by Olympias' flamboyant devotion to the orgiastic cult of Dionysios "with even wilder abandon than the others, and she would introduce into the festal procession numbers of large snakes, hand-tamed, which terrified the male spectators as they raised their heads from the wreaths of ivy . . . and twined themselves around the wands and garlands of the women."[1] She took this passion even further by sleeping with the divine serpents. Philip understandably found other beds more winning, which may explain why Alexander's only sibling by Olympias was a younger sister named Cleopatra. In any case, while Olympias was not jealous of these liaisons, she did resent their shameless openness. She happily tolerated the secondary wives acquired for diplomatic purposes. Threats to Alexander's position as heir, however, would bring out a bloody and ruthless fury. She was rumored to have addled the wits of another son of Philip, Arrhidaeus, by administering a dangerous drug.

As Olympias' resentments grew, she did not hesitate to use Alexander as a weapon to worry Philip. She spoiled the precocious child and fed him stories of his heroic lineage. His father's

Agaed line was said to be descended from Herakles, but her Epirot lineage was from Achilles, the ultimate hero of Greek history and myth, as well as from Helen of Troy. Olympias encouraged the identification with Achilles, heady stuff for a child, especially one like Alexander, who was already demonstrating superior qualities in childhood. It was doubly heady in that the child saw the heroic world of Achilles and the *Iliad* alive around him in the court and training grounds of Macedonia. Even more she confided in him—that he had been fathered by Zeus himself.

The child grew in no rarified court atmosphere, no closeted and stultifying harem. Life was heroic but not imperial. His mother and her women cooked and wove. Life in all its drama and rawness roared around him in the palace at Pella. Until the age of seven, Alexander was in the care of his nurse, Lanike. The energetic child must have been a severe trial to the nurse, but she had a good and loving heart; Alexander was to bear her a profound affection all of his life. Her brother, Cleitus the Black, was one of Philip's guards and an early role model in his life. It is easy to see the toddler and little boy reacting to the pacts of hunting dogs, the rough, boisterous clang of soldiers, and the sparks of honor with sheer wonder and delight. Alexander would have been an active presence, playing with his friends, imitating the soldiers. A beautiful and spirited child who showed an endless interest in them would have attracted the affection and admiration of these hard men. Already he was exhibiting the magnetism that would make him the talisman of victory for Macedonians.

Plutarch relates a story that at its core must relate an actual event. Philip was away reviewing the army when a Persian embassy arrived. The adolescent Alexander welcomed them and then proceeded to question them closely. His questions were those of a shrewd adult, not those of a child fascinated by the glitter of the Persian court. Alexander asked penetrating questions on the military capacity of the Persian Empire, its roads, and the military ability of its ruler. The envoys were amazed.

Philip had a prospective king to train, and by Alexander's seventh birthday took the boy's education firmly in hand. He appointed as Alexander's tutor a kinsman of Olympias, Leonidas. For Philip, however, Leonidas' chief qualification was that he was "a man of stern character," who placed the greatest emphasis on developing the boy's physical endurance. In later years Alexander would remark that Leonidas' idea of a light breakfast was a long night-march, and of supper, a light breakfast. He also remembered how his tutor inspected his possessions to see that Olympias had not slipped him an unnecessary indulgence. Leonidas' harsh school was the forge for Alexander's legendary physical hardiness and endurance. Admittedly, the future king had all the gifts of a great athlete, but it was the training that brought it out, developed, and tempered it into an instrument that would never fail him.

Leonidas' frugal nature once caused him to rebuke his pupil when the child threw two fistfuls of incense on the altar during sacrifice. "Alexander, when you have conquered the countries that produce these spices, you can make as extravagant sacrifices as you like: till then, don't waste it!" Years later, when Alexander had conquered Gaza, the spice trading center of Asia, he sent Leonidas a gift of eighteen tons of the precious stuff, enough to make him rich beyond the dreams of avarice. With it was a note from Alexander, "I have sent you plenty of myrrh and frankincense, so that you need not be stingy towards the gods any longer."[2] Alexander had a pithy sense of humor, but he also never forgot a slight.

While Leonidas hardened the boy, his second tutor provided companionship and affection. He was Lysimachus, a gentleman attached to Philip's court. Lysimachus deepened the link with Achilles that Olympias fostered by referring to Alexander as Achilles, himself as the hero's tutor, Phoenix, and Philip as Peleus, the hero's father. Alexander remained devoted to him and would one day risk his own life to save him.

The boy proved to be a phenomenally gifted student. He excelled in reading and writing. Later he would be known as someone who could read silently barely moving his lips, in an age when most people read out loud. He learned music and played the lyre with exceptional ability and feeling. The first historical reference to Alexander, in fact, concerns music. Athenian ambassadors noted that at a feast given by Philip for them, the ten-year-old Alexander played the lyre, and debated with another boy in their honor. Apparently he was too talented to suit Philip, who heard in his son's sweet-toned voice a trace of effeminacy. Philip rebuked him, saying that he should be ashamed to sing so well. Alexander never sang again; the insult was too deep. Despite this, he would have a lifelong delight in the performing and visual arts, and among his train would be the finest actors, musicians, and artists of the time.

Above all, Alexander excelled in the practice of arms—the sword, javelin, and the bow. He was an exceptionally swift runner, so talented that friends asked why he did not compete at the Olympic Games. Yet Alexander already had a marked distaste for the professional athletes that were ruining Greek sport. He felt he would be demeaned by running with them. He replied that he would run only if his competitors were kings. No one set the bar higher for Alexander than Alexander.

Like all highborn Macedonians, he was barely out of his mother's arms when he learned to ride. All his life he was a superb horseman, no easy feat in the days before the stirrup and firm saddle. Around one special horse, though, grew probably the most famous story of Alexander. He was at most ten when his father took him to see the warhorses offered him for sale. One outshadowed all the others, a pedigree stallion, all black but for a white blaze on the forehead in the shape of an oxhead, which gave him his name, Bucephalus. His owner asked an outrageous price, three times the most ever paid for a warhorse. But the horse was magnificent—big, powerful, and in his prime, rippling with nervous energy, uncontrollable, and wild. Philip was furious to be offered such an ungovernable animal. Alexander had his own opinion, and to his father's surprise openly stated it. "What a horse they are losing, and all because they don't know how to handle him, or dare not try!"

Again and again the boy stated his distress until Philip asked him, "Are you finding fault with your elders because you think you know more than they do, or can manage a horse better?"

"At least I can manage this one better," Alexander replied.

"And if you cannot, what penalty will you pay for being so impertinent?" asked Philip.

"I will pay the price of the horse," the boy replied.

The king's company burst out laughing, but Philip was game and confirmed the bet. Alexander went right up to the horse, took the bridle, and turned the animal toward the sun. He had seen that the animal was afraid of his own moving shadow. Then he ran along with the horse, stroking him to calm his fears. He sprang lightly upon his back and played easily with the reins to accustom the horse to his touch without tearing the mouth. Alexander felt the impatient power and unleashed him with a commanding voice and the light touch of his foot. Boy and beast disappeared in a cloud of dust down the field. Philip and his companions "held their breath and looked on in an agony of suspense" until Alexander reached the end of the course, turned the horse, and sped back in triumph and to the applause of the crowd. His father embraced and kissed him, tears streaming down his face, and said, "My boy, you must find a kingdom big enough for your ambitions. Macedonia is too small for you."[3]

Well might Philip have wept for joy. His son had demonstrated a bold confidence in himself and an instinctive resort to the decisive act. More than that was his determination to master both the powerful beast and the skepticism of the king and his companions. All of these qualities would have failed him had he not a natural and sensitive understanding of the horse and a body superbly equal to the task.

Between father and son there was genuine affection, but it was tempered at either extreme by Alexander's outright hero worship and his sense of competition. Philip was the excellent example of warrior and king. His influence is unmistakable as Alexander marched across Asia, from his ability to handle men, to his mastery of the arts of war, to his careful and just administration of growing empire. It is no wonder that Alexander's favorite line from the *Iliad* was "at the same time a good king and a strong spear-fighter."

Yet the sense of competition gnawed at the young prince. At the news of another success of Philip's, he would tell his friends, "Boys, my father will forestall me in everything. There will be nothing great or spectacular for you and me to show the world."[4] It was a critical age for the young, and Alexander freely indulged himself. His sense of rivalry with his father and his constant support of his mother in her war against Philip's slights merged into another complaint—that it was unseemly for Philip to be siring so many children with so many women. Word got to Philip, who unbraided his son, "Therefore, since you have so many rivals for the throne, prove yourself so brave and virtuous that you receive the kingship, not because I am who I am, but because you are who you are."[5] It was a telling rebuke. Philip knew exactly the effect he wanted to achieve. He must have recognized Alexander's growing compulsion to excel in everything he attempted, and the centrality it was assuming in his life. He had internalized Socrates' advice, "The nearest way to glory—a short cut, as it were—is to strive to be what you wish to be thought to be."[6] Years later while campaigning in Asia, Alexander would state, "I would rather excel the rest of mankind in my knowledge of what is best than in the extent of my power.[7]

Already a desire for fame was growing in the boy. Fame, in the Homeric world of the *Iliad* and Macedonia, was the measure of all manly things, the reward of excellence and work, and he would harness his entire being to this one single passion of his life. So channeled was he that amidst opportunity and examples of excess, he remained remarkably self-controlled and austere in his personal tastes. His father's vulgar excesses cannot but have reinforced this tendency.

Yoked with fame was another powerful force awakened in the young prince, a quality the Greeks called *pothos*, the yearning to seek what lay beyond vision and grasp. The embers of the *Iliad* had fallen on a rich and impressionable mind and had lighted a fire that would survive in legend long after his death. That mind was also animated by a devout religious sense, the legacy of his mother.

It was now clear to Philip that Alexander had outstripped his tutors. Philip's next step was worthy of a king, for he had a future king to prepare. He realized that Alexander needed more than a mere collection of skills to be a successful king. His intellect needed to be trained as rigorously as his body. For that Alexander would need philosophy in both its theoretical and practical senses—as Philip explained to his son, "So that you will not do the many things that I did and now regret."[8] Philip also realized that the boy could not be compelled to do anything but would accede to being led by good argument and logic. In other words, the boy had a firm but open mind.

Philip chose, from many applicants, Aristotle, the most famous pupil of Plato, and he arranged it with a kingly generosity. Philip earlier had destroyed Artistole's native city. Now he rebuilt it, gathered back its people, and added a handsome fee. Artistotle was worth the price and more. Into his hands Philip placed the twelve-year-old Alexander and a circle of friends and others of his age, mostly drawn from the sons of the great men of the kingdom. Macedonian kings ruled through their personal relationships with the great men of the kingdom, and this was the time to bond these future great men to Alexander. It would also serve Alexander to have men about him who had benefited from the same royal education.

Philip also shrewdly decided that the excitement of the court and army at Pella would be too much of a distraction and made available the groves and grottos of the sanctuary of the Nymphs near Mieza.

Alexander had already drunk deeply of the imagery and heroism of the *Iliad*. Under Aristotle's guidance, Homer's epic revealed its deeper truths, as the most profound study of men in war. The effect of Aristotle's examination of this book on the young Alexander should not be underestimated. Alexander "regarded the *Iliad* as a handbook of the art of war and took with him on his campaigns a text annotated by Aristotle, that became known as the 'the casket copy,' and which he always kept under his pillow together with his dagger."[9] The "casket" was the magnificent jeweled coffer that was taken as spoils after the Battle of Issus. So beautiful was it that it sparked a debate among his friends as to what precious thing to store in it. Alexander chose his *Iliad*.

Under Aristotle's guidance, Alexander's love of books blossomed. Euripides became his favorite playwright, and he learned large segments of his works by heart. Here, too, is an insight into his nature. Euripides was the first playwright to explore with compassion the fate of the vanquished and the treatment of women, something the hard-hearted Hellenes had not much concerned themselves with. There would be much of this compassion in Alexander the King.

Alexander also found, under Aristotle's tutelage, a deep love of medicine. During his campaigns, he was to be a frequent visitor to the field hospitals where he performed operations himself. This interest also may help explain the good health his armies consistently demonstrated. Aristotle also aroused in him a fascination with the natural and physical sciences, not unexpected of the world's first great scientist. It was an interest Alexander always maintained, taking numerous scientists with him to Asia in his train so that Artistotle would receive a continuous stream of specimens and artifacts.

The two years Alexander spent with Aristotle taught him how to think critically, "to put his faith in intellect."[10] Philip had given him the example of kingship, the *Iliad* had given him his ideals, and Leonidas had given him the tool of a robust body. Now all of these talents were harnessed to the intellect trained by Artistotle. The relationship has endlessly fascinated historians through the ages—the greatest mind of Hellas trained its greatest conqueror and most perfect prince. Intellectuals ever since have been trying to replicate that relationship by modestly instructing civilizations instead of kings. They failed to realize that the ingredients were the genius of thought and action, fused only where lightning strikes.

Chapter 3

The Warrior Prince

In 340 B.C., after two years in the groves of Mieza, Philip summoned Alexander and his friends back to Pella to the School of Royal Pages. For the first time in their lives, Philip and Alexander were in daily contact. Philip's dynastic ambitions do not fully explain the relationship between the two of them. Philip had always been pleased with Alexander. What father's heart would not rejoice in a son who could master Bucephalus? There was a real bond of affection that grew deeper as Philip now had direct charge of Alexander's training as his heir.

The boy was rapidly becoming a man, filling that form in which the world would remember him. He was below average height and of medium build, though tough and well muscled with a legendary iron constitution. His complexion was ruddy, and when exercised he face and chest would take a high color. His hair is variously described as blond or tawny. It was thick, and he wore it swept back and to the sides to resemble, as many said, a lion's mane. He was noted for cocking his head to the left and up as he listened, a dramatic and graceful pose that was studiously copied by his successors and sculptors alike. His voice was sharp and penetrating, and he spoke and walked quickly, features also copied by his successors. He had such a thin beard that he made a virtue of necessity by shaving, establishing a Western custom that lasted seven hundred years.

His eyes were said to be of different colors, one brown and the other gray or green. That alone would have arrested those who met him, but in the ancient world it was a magical sign of divine favor as well. What was truly magical was the look of the eyes. Contemporaries said they had a "melting" charm. There was no doubt that Alexander was one of the very few truly charismatic people to stride the earth. His father had that quality, as Demosthenes rued, but in Alexander it was an order of magnitude greater. Serving a man like that becomes intoxicating.

Two years later, in an extraordinary gesture of trust, Philip appointed the sixteen-year-old Alexander as regent and put the royal seal into his care as Philip left to campaign against Byzantium. Alexander was put to the test almost immediately when the Thracian tribe of the Maidoi, on the border of Paeonia and Thrace, revolted and threatened Philip's communications. Alexander marched immediately with the reserve and in a lightning campaign crushed the rebels, drove them from their city, and refounded it as a Macedonian settlement. He boldly gave the new city his own name—Alexandropolis (Alexander City). This act surely turned a few heads, for Alexander had unhesitatingly exercised a royal prerogative. It was a stunning performance for a sixteen-year-old and bore the hallmark of his future generalship—quickness of decision and speed of action.

Philip's reaction is unknown, but he kept in close touch with Alexander during his campaign, sending a stream of letters, closely advising his son both as father and king. From the tone of the letters, Philip still believed the young man had much to profit by his advice. He became particularly incensed when he discovered Alexander's clumsy attempts to bribe his way to the loyalty of certain Macedonians. A past master at bribery, he wrote, "What on earth gave you the deluded idea that you would ever make faithful friends out of those whose affections you had bought?"

Philip also was concerned that Alexander was not cultivating enough of the great sons of the Macedonian nobility since they would be his main support someday. There were too many young Greeks among his friends at that age. Friendship for Alexander was one of the great and manly virtues. It was to be exercised for itself and not necessarily for policy. Alexander was devoted to those to whom he had given his friendship. For him it was a highly personal relationship—the company of young men created an extraordinary bond not susceptible to clinical explanation, a relationship of enduring love and loyalty forged from the shared joys of exuberant youth, shared struggle, and shared loss.

Mary Renault pointed to deeper cause, the relentless conflict between his parents:

> That he kept his sanity he must have owed to his capacity for friendship, a solace he turned to while very young. Psychologically his face must have been his fortune; to this attractive boy people were drawn without the pretences of flattery, and his true child's instincts felt it. He grew up with a religious faith in friendship, making it a cult, publicly staking his life on it. The real loves of his life were friendships. . . . To be loved for himself, as he certainly often was, ministered to his constant need for reassurance, and he returned affection so warmly that it seldom let him down. When it did, it shook him to his roots. He had committed too much, and could not forgive.[1]

Alexander channeled his energies into his drive for glory and love of war. His emotional needs were for affection. If anything, he was indifferent to sex, saying once that it was sleep and sexual intercourse that, more than anything else, reminded him that he was mortal, equating both with the weakness of human nature. He also had an abhorrence of sexual abuse. When one of his officers offered to be the go-between for the purchase of beautiful slave boys, he flew into a rage and demanded repeatedly to know from his friends what shameful thing had ever been seen in him that this man should approach him so. He was equally harsh on those who abused women. On several occasions, he forcefully refused to take advantage of beautiful women that were loved by others. When Cassander, Antipater's son, whom Alexander detested, engaged in just such behavior, Alexander exclaimed, "It isn't allowable even to fall in love with anybody, because of you and people like you."[2]

At Mieza, the circle of Alexander's friends began to take shape and would be added to as time went on. Forever first among his friends was Hephestion, son of Amyntas, whose intellect had impressed Aristotle. Another was Ptolemy, son of Lagus, rumored to be Philip's bastard and Alexander's half-brother.

Philip's campaign was not going well, and within the year he summoned Alexander to him to subdue rebellious cities in southern Thrace. Returning in success, he found Philip fruitlessly besieging Potidea, his efforts consistently frustrated by Athenian naval power. It was probably in this siege that Alexander saved Philip's life when Philip's own mercenaries turned on him. A Greek had speared the king, who fell upon the ground. Philip feigned death as the mercenaries crowded around. Alexander came to his rescue, cut down the mercenaries around the king with his own hand, and protected him with his shield. Alexander remembered long after with some bitterness that his father had never acknowledged this act. Whatever was behind Philip's reluctance, it did not seem to affect his confidence in his son, which was deepened by their prolonged company and the absence of Olympias. Philip next sent Alexander back to Pella to resume the regency as he campaigned against the Scythians along the Danube. He was badly wounded by the Triballians who refused to give him passage home. Much of the administration of the kingdom thus fell on the prince.

Even in convalescence, Philip kept himself informed of the latest turns in Greek politics and found his opening. The Sacred League appealed to Philip to punish the Amphissaeans who had taken over some of Apollo's fields near Delphi. He agreed and instructed Alexander to mobilize the Macedonian host, but he put out the word that it was to be launched against the Illyrians. Philip's ruse worked too well. The Illyrians got wind of it and struck first. With the army assembled, Alexander counterpunched with the swiftness that was to become his hallmark. He was only seventeen. It was his third independent command, and he made it a small masterpiece. The Illyrians were tough, but Alexander handily defeated them and drove them back over the borders. It cannot have passed Philip's notice that his son had victoriously commanded the core of the Macedonian Army alone.

Now recovered, Philip marched. He turned the Theban garrison out of the Pass of Thermopylae and moved rapidly south. Demosthenes raised a panic in Athens, which then sought an anti-Macedonian alliance with Thebes. Arguing against the Macedonian ambassadors, Demosthenes offered up two cities tied to Athens by the most sacred treaties. One of them was Platea, the only city to have sent its spearmen to stand with the Athenians at Marathon. The craven depths to which the Athenian democracy had fallen would guarantee that Philip would not face the likes of men who had fought at Marathon. The Thebans accepted the offer and broke their treaty with Philip. Demosthenes had his war. Philip spent the winter fulfilling the League's mission and had succeeded by spring. He then sent an offer of peace that Demosthenes ensured was rejected. By late summer of 338 B.C., the hosts were facing each other near the Boeotian town of Chaeronea.

Both sides were roughly equal in strength: each had thirty thousand infantry and two thousand cavalry. The equality stopped there. The Greeks had no generals of note, and their troops consisted of citizens. The Macedonians were led by the greatest soldier of the age, and his army was the first truly professional, combined arms force in European history. The Greeks were arrayed with the Athenians on the left and the more experienced Thebans on the right. In the center were other lesser allies. Holding the anchor of the Greek right was the Theban Sacred Band, the most famous fighting formation in Greece, three-hundred-men-strong—pairs of lovers who vowed never to retreat. Philip commanded the Macedonian right personally. It was the place of honor, and he gave it the most difficult of tasks, one that required his own control. The phalanx was in the center. On the left he positioned his cavalry and gave command to Alexander, now eighteen-years-old, supported by experienced officers.

Philip's plan was simple and based upon a firm knowledge of his enemy. The Greeks were on good ground and the objective was to pull them out of that position. Philip began the battle by pitching into the Athenians with his Guard and then carefully withdrawing after a hard fight. One of the hardest maneuvers in warfare is a fighting retreat; it takes firm control and excellent troops. Philip had both. The Athenians, as he had expected, became disordered as they advanced. Their general cried out, "We won't stop until we've pushed the enemy back to Macedon"— and did nothing to bring order to his ranks. Philip observed, "Athenians do not know how to win."[3] As the giddy Athenians surged forward, their movement drew the units on their right flank after them and disrupted the entire line. Only the Theban Sacred Band maintained its post on the far right as the rest of the line was pulled forward. It was a post the Thebans could not desert for it hooked the Greek line onto a mountain and prevented an envelopment by the Macedonian cavalry opposite them.

Alexander's sense of timing was superb. He raised the paean, and the two thousand Macedonian and Thessalian cavalry surged forward with Alexander at their head. He had seen his father's personal heroism on the right and did not want to be outdone in valor. The cavalry wave struck among the Thebans. Alexander piled up corpses around himself, the living spearpoint of the Companion Cavalry. As the Theban phalanx disintegrated, their allies in the center followed under the impact of the phalanx. Alexander then turned on the Sacred Band and was the first to break into their ranks, a veritable fury. The Companions followed, and in the grim struggle that followed, cut down the entire band, not a man of whom deserted his post. The Thebans would erect a great stone lion over their mass grave. It stands guard to this day. Nearby, local people would name the tree under which the prince had cast his tent "Alexander's oak," which was still standing more than four hundred years later, according to Plutarch.

Philip turned on the Athenians just as Alexander led the cavalry forward and drove them back, the long sarissas of his phalanx stabbing death into their now-confused ranks. Somewhere in their rear rank, Demosthenes quailed. As the Athenian formation fell apart and fled, he was among those who threw away his shield to run faster. Written in gold on it were the words, "Good Fortune."

Philip called off the pursuit early to limit the butcher's bill for policy's sake. Nevertheless, both cities were thrown into deep mourning, each having lost at least a thousand dead; the Athenians lost another two thousand prisoners. Many Thebans were also captured. Signifying his victory, Philip set up a trophy, buried his dead, and thanked the gods. He was inordinately proud of Alexander, the hero of the day. He rejoiced as the men said, "Philip is our general, Alexander is our king." Rather than be jealous of his son, he was pleased that Alexander had won the love of the army, the guarantee of his rule once he followed Philip on the throne.

Philip also let his passions get the better of him, got drunk on unmixed wine, wreathed himself in celebration, and put on an arrogant display. Leading a parade among the Athenian corpses and past their prisoners, he mocked them and Demosthenes by chanting in rhyme the opening lines of the orator's speeches:

> "Son of Demosthenes, Demosthenes
> Of Paian deme, propose these."

From the ranks of the prisoners, the sharp voice of the orator, Demades, spoke: "King, when chance has given to you the opportunity to play the part of Agamemnon, are you not ashamed to take the role of Thersites?"[4] He hit his mark. Thersites was the common, mean-spirited buffoon in the *Iliad*. Philip instantly sobered up, and threw off his wreath and other symbols of victory. He marveled at the courage of Demades, freed him, and made him a member of his circle. Alexander was nowhere to be seen in this incident though surely he was an observer and must have recoiled at the humiliation of a valiant enemy. The Thebans Philip treated less well and placed a garrison in their city. The Athenians feared much worse and got much better. Their heralds were stunned at the terms. Athens would receive no garrison, nor would it lose its constitution; it was only to sign a treaty of alliance with Philip. Demades' influence won the release without ransom of the Athenian prisoners, and the ashes of their dead were returned under the escort of Alexander himself.

This would be Alexander's only visit to Athens, and it remained a pleasant memory. Like his father, he also fell in love with this city. Certainly he was treated royally to the point of obsequiousness. The Athenians voted statues of father and son on the Acropolis, and Alexander visited Plato's Academy. The visit was all too brief. Philip marched through the Peloponnesus in a show of strength and called an assembly of all the Greek states at Corinth. All came, save Sparta. The Council declared itself the League of Corinth and gave Philip the object of his twenty years' struggle. He was declared Hegemon, warleader of the Greeks, and empowered to launch a war of revenge against the Persians.

For the first time in his reign, Philip found no enemies at hand, and upon his return to Macedonia, his eye fell upon Cleopatra, the beautiful niece of the Companion lord, Attalus. He determined to marry her and set in train the events that would sunder the royal family. This marriage was an affront to Olympias, and that meant Alexander felt it as well. However, Alexander determined to attend the wedding feast if only to emphasize his position as heir and Olympias' as queen mother. Loyalty and comradeship had their price. He owed his father that. Still, he was primed to find an insult.

It was not long in coming. Macedonian feasts quickly degenerated into roaring drunks, and this was no exception. Attalus proposed a toast to Philip and his bride that they might produce a true-blooded Macedonian heir. Alexander shot to his feet at this deadliest of insults, and shouted, "Villain, do you take me for a bastard, then?" With that, he threw a cup at Attalus' head. Philip struggled to his feet, enraged at the affront to his guest. Violent words were exchanged, so fiery that Philip drew his sword on Alexander and advanced upon him. Tipsy and with a bad leg, he stumbled and went crashing to the floor amid overturned tables and spilled wine. Alexander stood there and said, "Here is the man who was making ready to cross from Europe to Asia, and who cannot even cross from one table to another without losing his balance."[5]

Alexander's friends dragged him away to cool down in the wake of so many killing words. He acted quickly before Philip could gather his wits and took his mother swiftly to Epirus and the safety of her brother's palace. He himself disappeared into the wilds of Illyria. Of his stay there we know nothing. Philip could not have missed the dangerous implications of an able and disaffected prince among his ancient enemies while he was preparing to invade the Persian Empire. He was lucky that one of his closest friends had the loyalty to bring him to his senses. Demaratus the Corinthian had come to visit, and Philip asked him about affairs in Greece. Demaratus instead said, "It is all very well for you to show so much concern for the affairs of Greece, Philip. How about the disharmony you have brought about in our own household?" Again a word of reproof had awakened Philip's better nature and his common sense. He sent Demaratus as his go-between, who convinced the prince to return.

The two were reconciled, but their relationship was never the same. The tension over Philip's marriage had not disappeared, and Alexander's sensitivity to slight remained high. The fortunes of Attalus and his faction were ascendant, a constant reminder of the insult at the feast. Any new threat to his position could push him beyond the rational. The opportunity came quickly enough. Alexander got wind that Philip was planning an important marriage for his son, Arrihidaeus, to the daughter of the Persian satrap and king of Caria, Pixodorus. The marriage would have secured an important ally in Asia Minor when Philip began his campaign. Alexander got wind of it and failed to see in it merely the move of a pawn. He was disposed to think the worst, that he was being supplanted by his brother. He was ill served by his mother and his friends who encouraged him in this. The state of his mind can be guessed in that he seriously thought Philip would replace him with a half-wit. He threw judgment to the winds and sent to Pixodorus to inform him of the unsuitability of his bastard brother and offer himself as the bridegroom. The plot was revealed to Philip who marched into Alexander's room with Philotas, one of Alexander's companions and son of Parmenion, as a witness. "There he scolded his son and angrily reproached him for behaving so ignobly and so unworthily of his position as to wish to marry the daughter of a mere Carian, who was no more than a slave of a barbarian king."[6] Philotas may have been the informer. Surely there was one in Alexander's company, for his other friends were exiled for their part in the affair. Only Hephestion he exempted as a good influence. But Philip was not through rubbing Alexander's nose in his foolishness. He ordered Alexander's emissary, the great actor Thettalus, brought from Corinth in chains. The sight of one of his friends suffering for him must surely have scalded Alexander's pride beyond bearing. In the meantime, Philip had begun his war by dispatching Parmenion and Attalus in the spring of 336 B.C. with the advance guard of the army to Asia Minor. Philip's short leash on Alexander was pulled even tighter when he kept his son at home, mired in shame.

As the same time, Philip announced another marriage. Not his, this time, but that of Cleopatra—his daughter by Olympias and Alexander's younger sister—to Olympias' brother, Alexander, King of Epirus. That fall he hosted a great celebration of his rule that attracted envoys and guests from all of Greece. Philip wanted to use the opportunity to refute the allegations that he was a tyrant by appearing without bodyguards, the emblems of a tyrant.

It was Philip's hour of supreme good fortune, but the price of excess had come due. His chief bodyguard, Pausanias, felt wronged to the core of his soul. He had been Philip's lover as a younger man and had caused the death of another of Philip's lovers, a client of Attalus. Avenging the dead young man, Attalus had got Pausanias drunk and then turned him over to his stable hands to be raped. Pausanias had gone for redress to Philip who had given him land and position, but not what he wanted most, the punishment of Attalus. Now with the star of Attalus high, the wound in Pausanias' honor bled constantly. He turned his hatred on Philip.

The day of the festival, Philip entered the theater escorted by the two Alexanders, son and son-in-law. Then he bade them take their seats so he could walk unassisted and unguarded to his throne. He had not taken more than a few steps when Pausanias rushed upon him and drove a dagger between his ribs. Philip fell dead, and his assassin ran out to the horses waiting for him. He tripped on a vine and lost his head start; as he rose, the rest of the bodyguards were upon him, stabbing with their javelins.

Chapter 4

"My Son, You Are Invincible!"

ALEXANDER HAD WITNESSED the assassin's blow from his seat next to Philip's throne. His father's officers rushed to his protection and escorted him to the palace where they declared him king. He acted swiftly to secure the crown in a wave of executions that eliminated both rivals and supposed conspirators. Antiquity absolved him of his father's murder; there was no evidence, and the religious nature of Alexander would have recoiled at patricide, the foulest crime known to the Hellenic world.

More fingers pointed to Olympias, who saw the marriage of her daughter as a threat to her own position. Philip could have shed his troublesome queen now that he had a daughter to bind Epirus to Macedonia. She did her reputation no good by boldly paying extraordinary honors to the memory of the assassin. More damning evidence pointed to Demosthenes as a conspirator. Ever to be the first with good news, he publicly announced the news of Philip's death long before news could have reached Athens. At the same time, he was found to be in communication with Attalus in Asia Minor, attempting to suborn his allegiance.

This correspondence was his death sentence. Demosthenes' efforts were also financed by the new Persian monarch, Darius III, whose realm Philip had already invaded. The Great King had good reasons to see him dead.[1]

It took more than executions to secure a crown, and Alexander quickly impressed the Macedonians by his good sense and tact. He stated that only the name of the king had changed, and that the principles of Philip's kingship would remain. Alexander also kept the army busy with constant tactical exercises and practice at arms. Discipline was tightened.

Athens immediately agitated to throw off Macedonian leadership, and many states followed. Even Thessaly wavered. Alexander lost no time to halt the stampede. First he descended into Thessaly with his army to receive the archonship that had been his father's. Next he won over many of the Greeks through the mildness of his diplomacy. The rest he overawed by appearing outside Thebes with the full Macedonian army after forced marches. He said, "Demosthenes called me a boy while I was in Illyria and among the Triballi, and a youth when I was marching through Thessaly; I will show him I am a man by the time I reach the walls of Athens."[2] Thebes panicked, and the panic rushed south to Athens as well, which sent envoys to beg forgiveness for the tardy recognition of his leadership. Demosthenes was part of the delegation, but turned back before reaching Alexander, probably for good reason. Again Alexander calmed the Athenians. He then convened a council of the Corinthian League that quickly awarded him his father's office as Hegemon in the war of revenge against Persia.

Alexander's effort to secure his position was a tour de force for anyone. For a twenty-year-old, it was simply astounding. He had operated astutely on political, diplomatic, and military lines all at the same time. His grasp of the situation and judgment were uncanny. All of his efforts were brought to a synergistic perfection by his decisiveness and speed of action.

With the situation now in hand, Alexander returned to Macedonia by way of Delphi where he asked for an oracle on his upcoming expedition against the Persians from the priestess of Apollo. She protested that it was not the day for oracles, whereupon he lifted her bodily and carried her to the shrine. She exclaimed, "My son, you are invincible!" He set her down, saying that she had given him the prophecy he wanted.[3] The Greek word for invincible was *anikitos,* which became his favorite epithet.

By the next spring in 335 B.C., the Illyrian and Thracian tribes to the west and north threw off their allegiance, posing a direct threat to communications with the advance guard in Asia Minor. Alexander's advisers recommended negotiations, but he saw that a demonstration of Macedonian power would be more effective. His army sped north, subduing one tribe after another, all the way to the Danube, where he dealt a crushing defeat to the Triballians, the same tribe that had recently bested Philip. He encountered no challenge beyond his grasp. On one occasion when the Triballians guarding a pass rolled carts down on Alexander's phalanx, he ordered the men to fall on the ground and cover themselves with their shields. Not a man was lost as the carts bounced over them. For the first time, the historians speak of his *pothos* as he approached the Danube. It was a challenge to be met, a line to be crossed. He made a highly efficient river crossing supported by galleys he had had sent up through the Black Sea that showed a very high order of planning and coordination. So dramatic was the crossing that the Thracian Getae fled without a fight. He recrossed the river without a casualty and received the embassies of suddenly friendly tribes. Even the distant Celts sent an embassy. They towered above Alexander and boasted in response to his question that they feared nothing but that the sky should fall on them. He surely must have enjoyed the bravado.

On the Danube, he heard that the Illyrians in the west had revolted. He marched so quickly upon them that he interrupted a human sacrifice they were conducting outside their main fort of Pelion. He came to the rescue of one of his detached elements but was in turn trapped in the narrow passes. He dazzled the barbarians by a show of Macedonian drill that so unnerved them, they fled. On another occasion, he was pressed hard as his forces were crossing a river. He deployed his archers to midstream and assembled his catapults on the far bank to provide support, the first recorded use of artillery in the field, rather than in siege. He crushed the Illyrians by a night march on their sleeping armies outside their capital. So firmly did he settle these borders that they saw no unrest for the remainder of his life. It would be difficult to find a set of campaigns in which a commander demonstrated such a blend of tactical innovation, long-term planning, speed, psychological operations, and instinct for the jugular.

In his absence, the Great King's gold had been unraveling the ever-loose allegiance of the Greeks. Demosthenes pocketed a huge sum of three hundred talents, spread rumors that Alexander had died in the north, and encouraged the Thebans to throw out the Macedonian. They only succeeded in shutting the garrison up in the citadel. More fatally, they had committed an act of rebellion against the League of which Alexander was Hegemon, giving him every legal and moral authority to act against them.

He received the news in newly captured Pelion. It was three hundred miles to Thebes, and his army badly needed a rest, but the gravity of the situation made time the critical factor. In thirteen days of forced marches, Alexander debouched, to the shock of the Thebans, outside their city again. He offered them the opportunity to return to their allegiance to the League. They refused and sent an insulting reply. He moved his army opposite the Electra Gate and once more offered them terms. Instead the Theban army issued from the city and drove in his outposts. He saw his chance and counterattacked, driving the Thebans back through the gate. In the confusion, the Macedonians pushed through the gate as well, and Thebes was lost. More than six thousand Theban men fell in the ensuing slaughter and sack. The League voted Thebes' punishment, surely with Alexander's approval. The surviving population, more than thirty thousand, was sold off into slavery and the city razed. It was an object lesson in Macedonian frightfulness, and it succeeded. All Greece was supine in terror at the fate of one of its great cities. The Athenians came crawling again. At first Alexander demanded the surrender of Demosthenes and other anti-Macedonian orators, but Demades inter-vened, and Alexander relented. He could not afford to drive the Athenians to desperation when his war against Persia beckoned. Policy came before revenge.

Alexander spared the temples and the home of the great poet Pindar. In later years he came to regret the destruction of the city, and freed every Theban he could find. He also was capable of the grand gesture, especially when it concerned women. Apparently his standing orders forbade violence to women even in the horrors of a fallen city. His Thracian auxiliaries brought to him for judgment a Theban woman who had killed their officer. She explained that he had raped her, then demanded her gold. She told him it was hidden in the well, and when he peered over the edge she hit him with a tile and threw him in to drown. Alexander instantly recognized a woman of spirit and asked who she was. She replied that her name was Timocleia, and said, "I am the sister of Theagenes who commanded our army against your father at Chaeronea fighting for the liberty of Greece." Filled with admiration of her courage, he freed her and her children on the spot.[4]

He spent the winter in Macedonia making final preparations for the war. He decided to leave Antipater as regent of Macedonia and deputy Hegemon with a small army. Parmenion would be his second-in-command on the expedition. Their combined force would be thirty thousand infantry and more than five thousand cavalry. The fact that he was hugely in debt with a near-empty treasury did not daunt him. As he was about to board his ship for Asia, he inquired of his Companions if any were in need and settled upon them almost all his estates and properties. Perdiccas asked, "But your majesty, what are you leaving for yourself?"

"My hopes," said Alexander.

"Very well, then, those who serve with you will share those too," replied Perdiccas who refused Alexander's gift as did his other friends. To others he gave away all he had. Pouring a libation into the Hellespont, he tossed in the golden cup and sailed.[5]

Chapter 5

Won by the Spear

A s alexander's galley crossed the Hellespont and approached the Troad, he cast a spear into the shore and was the first to leap into Asia, "signifying that he received Asia from the gods as a spear-won prize."[1] It was a typical dramatic gesture for Alexander who never let slip the opportunity to win his victories first in the minds of men. That is much of the battle.

With his armies united, his first act was to travel the short distance to the site of ancient Troy where he

> sacrificed to Athena and poured libations to the heroes of the Greek Army. He anointed with oil the column which marks the grave of Achilles, ran a race by it naked with his companions, as the custom is, and then crowned it with a wreath: he remarked that Achilles was happy in having found a faithful friend while he lived and a great poet to sing of his deeds after his death.[2]

By honoring the Greek heroes before Troy, he was drawing parallels to the cycles of war between Greece and Asia, of which the Persian invasions of the past were only the latest episodes. He was also drawing a parallel with the Greek victory over Troy. The priest of Athena gave him a prophecy of victory. In return, Alexander made a great sacrifice, dedicated his own armor to the goddess, and in exchange took the finest panoply deposited in the sanctuary of the goddess.

Already his reputation had caused the satraps of Asia Minor to assemble their forces nearby to offer battle. They had ignored as beneath their dignity the good advice of the Greek mercenary general, Memnon, to avoid a pitched battle but instead carry the war to Macedonia, a strategy made easy by the vaster naval assets of the Great King. Alexander found them positioned on the other side of the swift-flowing Granicus River. They had twenty thousand cavalry, five thousand Greek mercenaries, and perhaps fifteen thousand infantry levies of poor quality. Alexander approached with about nineteen thousand men.[3]

It was the Macedonian month of Daesius, a month in which Macedonian kings never fought, his officers reminded him. Alexander ordered the name of the month changed on the spot. Parmenion advised him to wait until the next morning, but Alexander replied that the Hellespont would blush for shame if Alexander, after crossing it would be afraid to cross this small river. "Such hesitancy would be unworthy of the fighting fame of our people and of my own promptitude in the face of danger. Without doubt it would give the Persians added confidence; nothing has yet happened to them to cause them alarm, and they would begin to think they were as good soldiers as we."[4] In these few words, he had explained the vital necessity of seizing the moral ascendancy over an enemy.

Alexander's determination to force a battle was not the product of headstrong youth. He was demonstrating the "the ability to assess the situation at a glance."[5] This quality is called *coup d'oeil*, stroke of the eye in French. It is an innate gift of the great commander. He had seen that the Persians had made a fatal deployment by placing their cavalry along the riverbank. Cavalry's great value is in its momentum and maneuverability. The Persians had deprived their cavalry of both. The stationary horse made a very poor fighting platform. He had also seen that the Persians had stationed their formidable Greek mercenary infantry too far to the rear to intervene. Finally, he had identified the cluster of Persian leaders in the center of their line.

Action followed swiftly. He sent Parmenion to command the left and then positioned himself on the right with the Companions and light troops. To his left were the Guards, the regiments of the phalanx, and finally the Thessalian cavalry supported by more light troops. A profound hush settled over both banks of the river as the armies waited. Alexander cut thru the silence, leaping onto his horse and shouting to his guard "to play the man." He ordered a mixed strike force of Companions, lancers, and light cavalry to charge first. As they splashed across the river under a hail of Persian arrows and javelins, Alexander plunged into the river followed by thirteen squadrons of his Companions. His strike force had concentrated the attention of the Persians in a desperate fight up the muddy bank while Alexander led his Companions upstream against the swift current to cut obliquely toward the other bank. Arrian says this was to avoid being attacked in the flank. The oblique approach allowed Alexander to transform his column by a right turn into a line that struck along the enemy left flank. It was a tricky maneuver, but the Companions were up to it.

The surprised Persians were at a disadvantage with their javelins against the long cornel wood lances of the Companions. A wave of thrusting lances bloodied the Persian defenders and pushed them back from the bank. Soon the press of masses of cavalry cramped the Macedonians' use of their lances or broke them, and the battle became hand-to-hand with swords and axes. As more and more Persians shifted toward Alexander, the strike force was able to secure its position on the bank as well.

Resplendent in his armor and white plumed helmet, Alexander was in the thick of the fighting. He broke a lance as he left its point in a corpse and called to his groom for another, but the man had splintered his as well though he continued to use its butt to good effect. Alexander called for another and was given one by Demaratus, the Corinthian, one of his bodyguards. At this moment, Alexander saw Mithridates, the Great King's son-in-law riding ahead of a wedged-shaped body of men into the fight. Alexander picked him out, spurred his horse in advance of his own men, and drove his lance full into Mithradates' face. A shout of triumph rose from the Macedonians at the sight of the feat. As the man hit the ground, Rhoesaces, brother of Spithradates, the Persian commander, rode up to avenge him. He struck Alexander from the side with an ax, sheering away one of his white plumes and lying open the helmet itself. His helmet gone, bleeding from a minor scalp wound, and his head surely ringing from the blow, Alexander was still self-possessed enough to wheel his horse about and run Rhoesaces through with his lance. As Alexander pulled the lance from the corpse, Spithradates rode up behind Alexander, his arm raised for the killing blow. History held its breath in that moment. But Cleitus the Black, commander of the Royal Squadron of the Companion Cavalry, had spurred forward and with a single blow of his heavy sword severed the Persian's arm at the shoulder.

As Alexander began the action on the right, the phalanx in the center had crossed the river, and with their hedge of pikes drove off the cavalry. Now shorn of many of its leaders, the Persian cavalry fled the field. The Greek mercenaries asked for quarter, but Alexander's blood was up, and he refused. He led the charge into them and lost his horse to a sword thrust in the belly. Alexander lost more men in this part of the battle than with the Persian cavalry because he was fighting hardened professionals made desperate. Perhaps his passion was another more calculated example of the object lesson. He knew that Greek mercenaries were the most effective troops the Persians had because the constant disorder of Greece had driven tens of thousands of Greeks into Persian service. By refusing quarter, he was following the Corinthian League's ruling that continued service with the Persians was treason to their fatherland. In the future, since the alternative was established, he was all too happy to accept the surrender of such men into his own service.

The day after the battle, he buried his dead with their arms and equipment and ordered that their children be given immunity from taxes. The dead Persians and mercenaries he also gave decent burial. He visited the wounded, asked how their injuries were earned, and allowed them to brag as much as they wanted of their deeds. As thanks to Athena for her armor and shield, he sent three hundred Persian panoplies to Athens with the dedication: "Alexander, son of Philip, and the Greeks (except the Lacedaemonians) dedicated these spoils, taken from the Persians who dwell in Asia."[6] He would not miss an opportunity to shore up Athenian support and shame the Spartans.

The immediate effect of the battle was dramatic. The loss of so many satraps stripped the Persians of leadership in Asia Minor. The Greek cities along the Aegean, long subject to the Great King, eagerly opened their gates to Alexander. Even Sardis, once the capital of King Croesus of Lydia, and now the main Persian base in the Aegean, surrendered. Only Miletus and Halicarnassus held out tenaciously under the command of Memnon, but both were eventually reduced. Alexander was again well served by fortune when Memnon died suddenly, removing the most formidable of Darius' generals. At this time, Alexander dismissed his fleet. He could not bear its expense and, since it was inferior to the Persian fleet, not much good in any case. Also he thought to give his army no hope of escape, but only the prospect of victory or death. He had another plan for the Persian fleet.

One by one, Alexander reduced the rich regions of western and southern Asia Minor. At Gordium, capital of Phrygia, reputed to be the home of the legendary King Midas, he was shown the greatest puzzle of antiquity: a chariot whose yoke was bound with the most intricate of knots that no one had ever been able to untie. Prophecy predicted that he who could untie this Gordian Knot would rule Asia. The story attracted Alexander like a magnet; it was a supreme challenge, redolent with the prospect of divine favor. After examining it for a moment, he drew his sword and sliced through the knots, signaling exactly how Asia would be won. Another source states he simply removed the pin that held the yoke to the chariot pole and then drew out the yoke itself. In either case, he had arrived at an original solution and added momentum to the belief in his divine favor and the inevitability of his victory.

Next he marched on Cilicia, that fertile corner where Asia Minor and Syria meet. The Persians strongly held a vital pass into the region called the Cilician Gates. Alexander sent Parmenion forward with the main army while he enveloped the position with his light infantry. The movement was discovered, but his reputation had preceded him, and the Persians fled at the news that Alexander himself was leading the encircling force. He entered Cilicia unopposed, and then stopped there for months. One day, after becoming overheated through exercise, he plunged into the icy waters of a river and immediately went into convulsions followed by fever. The recovery was extended but offered an example of Alexander's unshakable trust in his circle of friends—in this case, Philip of Acarnania, his physician. As Philip handed him a cup with his medication, Alexander read a letter from Parmenion warning him that Philip intended to poison him. He gave the letter to Philip and drank the medicine as his friend read the warning. Philip exclaimed, "The charge of murder that has been brought against me will be repudiated by your recovery." He implored Alexander to put his mind at ease and let the medicine work.

Alexander was overcome with emotion and replied, "Philip, if the gods had granted you the ideal method of testing my feelings towards you . . . you could not have hoped for one better than this. Even though I received this letter, I still drank the potion you had made up, and now you must believe that I am as concerned about clearing your name as I am for my recovery." Then he offered his right hand.[7]

Curtius, who related this incident, then took the opportunity to explore the hold Alexander had those around him:

> The Macedonians have a natural tendency to venerate their royalty, but even taking that into account, the extent of their admiration, or their burning affection, for this particular king is difficult to de-

scribe. First of all, they thought his every enterprise had divine aid. Fortune was with him at every turn and so even his rashness had produced glorious results. His age gave added luster to all his achievements for, though hardly old enough for undertakings of such magnitude, he was well up to them. Then there are the things generally regarded as rather unimportant but which tend to find greater approval among soldiers: the fact that he exercised with his men, that he made his appearance and dress little different from the ordinary citizen's, that he had the energy of a soldier. Whether these characteristics were natural or consciously cultivated, they had made him in the eyes of his men as much an object of affection as awe.[8]

That awe was expressed in absolute devotion. Curtius was correct when he said it was Alexander's nature as a man and a soldier that was so powerful. Male bonding has no more powerful example in history. Alexander never asked his men to do what he would not do himself, and his exploits set the shining example for courage. He also set the standard for excellence in all endeavors. Once when he rode up the front of his army before a battle, he saw a man still adjusting his javelin strap. Alexander dismounted, rushed into the ranks, and pushed the man out through the rear of the formation, saying he wanted no sluggards in his army.

He always cared for the well-being and health of his men and visited the wounded immediately after a battle. Nothing improves the morale of an army than to know that the care of the wounded is a priority. The care of the dead was equally important, and Alexander never failed to honor them, such as the day after the battle at Issus when "he also gave a splendid military funeral to the dead in the presence of the whole army paraded in full war equipment. At the ceremony he spoke in praise of every man who by his own observation or from reliable report he knew had distinguished himself in the fighting, and marked his approval each case by a suitable reward."[9] Maj. Gen. J. F. C. Fuller, one of the most perceptive soldiers of the modern age, also points out that "[w]hat appealed to his men probably more than anything else was his unexpected kindness towards them."[10]

During his first winter in Asia, he sent the newly married men home until the spring. Toward the end of his life, he took extraordinary care to see that his returning veterans were well cared for and declared that the children of his fallen soldiers would continue to receive their fathers' pay. He was known to warm half-frozen men by the fire in his own chair. On one occasion, he encountered one of his men bending under the weight of an enormous load of gold being transported from a Persian treasury. Alexander encouraged the man that if he could make it to the camp, the load was his.

The total effect was miraculous. As Fuller concludes, "Incidents such as these bound his men to him with invisible and unbreakable moral ties. They endowed them with particles of his invincible will, and, under his leadership, they obliterated dangers, smoothed away adversities, and enabled him to lead them to what for them appeared to be the ends of the world."[11]

Darius heard only that Alexander was immobilized in Cilicia, preferring to believe it was fear to meet his huge host gathered and waiting on the plains of Assyria. Since Darius was not the most decisive of monarchs, his opinion swayed back and forth with the recommendations of his courtiers. None of them were eager to be too frank, especially after he had executed the Athenian general, Charidemus, who had given him excellent advice but advice he thought demeaning to his dignity: he had suggested Darius not risk his person in battle but send a large force under a proven general. That aroused Darius' suspicions that the Athenian wanted the command for himself so that he could betray it to Alexander—yet the man had been on Alexander's wanted list after the fall of Thebes. This was an indication that all the gold Darius had spent on Demosthenes had not bought him useful intelligence. After Charidemus was hauled away to execution, the flow of advice naturally was for the Great King to command in person, which had led to his army's stationary position in Assyria. A Macedonian traitor advised him to stay where he was because the open ground would allow him to maneuver his entire force. He argued, from firsthand knowledge of

Alexander, that the Macedonian king was certainly not hiding from him. "Your majesty need have no fears on that score. Alexander will march against you, in fact he is probably on his way now." This advice, Darius also disregarded, and out of sheer nervousness he moved on Alexander.[12]

The traitor had been right. Alexander was now looking for Darius. He headed south for the pass through the mountains that paralleled the coast. At this point he lost track of Darius and thought him still at a forward base to the east of the mountains. Instead, Darius had inadvertently seized the initiative and marched through a more northern pass that led straight into Cilicia. He had cut Alexander's communications and taken his hospital at Issus, mutilating and then killing all of the Macedonian sick and injured. Alexander was astounded when he heard the news that Darius lay upon his rear but instantly recognized the inherent opportunities of the changed situation. He gathered his senior officers together and delivered one of the great fighting speeches in history, one that he knew would be retransmitted through the ranks.

> Remember that already danger has often threatened you and you have looked at it triumphantly in the face; this time the struggle will be between a victorious army and an enemy already once vanquished. God himself, moreover, by suggesting to Darius to leave the open ground and cram his great army into a confined space, has taken charge of operations on our behalf. We ourselves shall have room enough to deploy our infantry, while they, no match for us either in bodily strength or resolution, will find their superiority in numbers of no avail. Our enemies are Medes and Persians, men who for centuries have lived soft and luxurious lives; we of Macedon for generations past have been trained in the hard school of danger and war. Above all, we are free men, and they are slaves. There are Greek troops, to be sure, in Persian service—but how different is their cause from ours! They will be fighting for pay—and not much of it at that; we, on the contrary, shall fight for Greece, and our hearts will be in it. As for our foreign troops—Thracians, Paeonians, Illyrians, Agrianes—they are the best and stoutest soldiers in Europe, and they will find as their opponents the slackest and soft-

est tribes of Asia. And what, finally, of the two men in supreme command? You have Alexander, they—Darius![13]

He spoke of the riches to be gained in this battle, that this would be the contest for the sovereignty of Asia for the Great King, and that the flower of Darius' nation were on the field. He reminded them of their shared struggles and triumphs and named each man conspicuous for his deeds. He alluded tactfully to his own deeds and the wounds he had suffered to remind them that he had shared every danger with them. Then he spoke of Xenophon and the Ten Thousand Greeks and how they had bested the might of the Great King with a smaller and weaker force. Finally, he encouraged their valor in ringing terms that reached an emotional crescendo when his officers crowded around him to grasp his hand and beg him to lead them on without delay. It was a masterful motivational performance that infused his leaders with Alexander's own implacable will to victory.

He ordered the men fed, then quickly turned the army about and marched north up the coast. Darius had handed him a great gift—to fight on a narrow coastal plain that would negate his numbers. Alexander, by his boldness of conception and action, had snatched back the initiative. As the plain expanded before him, he put his army in battle array and marched north with the sea on his left and the mountains brushing his right. The late October weather was perfect. It was 333 B.C., a bare eighteen months since Alexander had thrown his spear into the earth of the Troad. The showdown had come.

He found Darius' unwieldy host behind the Pinarus River and noted that in places the Persians had palisaded the far bank where it was easy to mount. Men who automatically threw up defenses were already half-beaten. He took in Darius' plan at a glance. In the center Darius had placed his twelve thousand Greek mercenaries, supported by five thousand Persian infantry on either flank. The left was all light infantry. On his right he had massed his huge numbers of cavalry with the obvious intention of crushing Alexander's sea flank and enveloping the phalanx in Alexander's center. Darius had heard much of the deadly

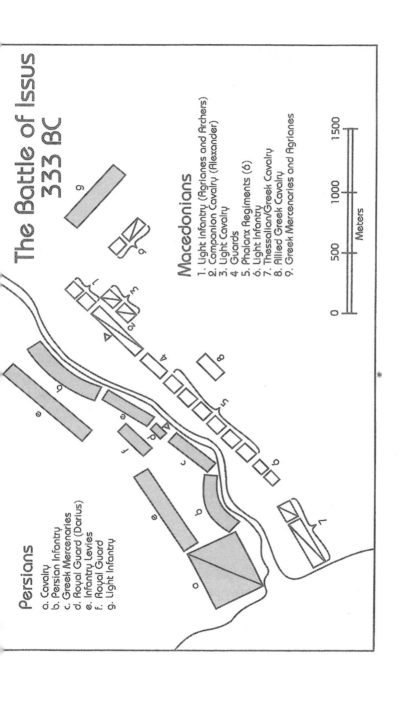

The Battle of Issus 333 BC

Persians
a. Cavalry
b. Persian Infantry
c. Greek Mercenaries
d. Royal Guard (Darius)
e. Infantry Levies
f. Royal Guard
g. Light Infantry

Macedonians
1. Light Infantry (Agrianes and Archers)
2. Companion Cavalry (Alexander)
3. Light Cavalry
4. Guards
5. Phalanx Regiments (6)
6. Light Infantry
7. Thessalian/Greek Cavalry
8. Allied Greek Cavalry
9. Greek Mercenaries and Agrianes

0   500   1000   1500

Meters

hedge of sarissa points and identified it as Alexander's center of gravity. Of course, it was a mistake. Alexander was Alexander's center of gravity. On his left Darius placed light infantry on the slopes of the mountains to be able to fall upon Alexander's right. Other useless masses of troops were stacked up behind the Persian front. Darius took the traditional place of the Persian kings in the center with his two thousand royal guards, the famed *Melophoroi* or Apple-Bearers from the golden apples forming the butt of their spears. Darius may well have had as many as eighty thousand men, including at least twenty-four thousand cavalry, the maximum that could have been supplied under ancient conditions. Alexander had at most nineteen thousand men, of which five thousand were cavalry. He was outnumbered by at least three to one.[14]

Alexander came up with his Companion Cavalry on his right, the phalanx in the center, and the Thessalian and allied cavalry on the left under the command of Parmenion. His Hypaspists formed the flexible hinge between the phalanx and the Companions. To the right of his Companions, he placed his light troops to counter the Persian light troops now above them on the slopes. His first action was to strike at these Persians. They quickly fled up the slopes and would be no further trouble. Alexander left a few hundred horsemen to observe and drew his light troops closer to his right.

Alexander now very deliberately drew his army toward the river, halting it to ride up the line offering encouragement to each unit; singling out for praise the deeds of the brave men he knew everywhere. Only a soldier will know what wings are given to the spirit when the commander singles out men by name to praise for their valor. He had a photographic memory and could recall thousands of names and biographies at will. His officers had done their work well, and now he had whipped up their enthusiasm till they shouted as he passed, "Wait no longer—forward to the assault!"[15]

With a snarl, the Macedonians broke into their unearthly paean; the Persians followed with theirs, and the trumpets of both sides added to the din till the air rang from the mountains to the sea. Before the echoes had faded, Alexander led his Companions in a charge across the river at the Persian left. The speed of the advance negated the effect of the Persian arrows, which arced up from their ranks in such numbers that they collided in air, breaking their momentum and impact. The Persian left wavered as the Companions, Alexander at their head, smashed into them. The phalanx in the center, however, became disorganized in crossing the river and was held up either by the steepness of the bank or the palisades. Gaps opened up in its ranks into which the Greek mercenaries attacked. In the desperate fighting on the muddy bank and in the shallows, 120 Macedonians fell. Simultaneously as Alexander charged, the great mass of Persian cavalry on their right advanced through the river to crash into the Thessalian and allied cavalry, running down an entire squadron with their impact. The battle had reached a critical point—the phalanx in the center struggled with the Greek mercenaries to surmount the bank, and the cavalry on the left was barely able to hold its own. On the right, however, Alexander had put to flight the mass of Persian light infantry. Now he turned on the Persian center.

Darius had been his target all along. The Great King in his gilded chariot towered in the center, big man that he was, and was immediately the magnet of every Macedonian eager for the glory of striking him down. The fighting surged toward him, and his guardsmen fell in heaps around him. His own brother, Oxathres, threw himself between Darius and the Macedonians, cutting down many who approached the royal chariot. The stabbing cornel wood lances of the Macedonians quickly thinned the guardsmen around Darius, despite his brother's heroism. His horses were wounded and unmanageable and threatened to bolt into the Macedonian ranks. The driver must have fallen dead, for Darius was forced to violate tradition and try and control the hysterical team himself.

Alexander, his helmet gone, was now upon him, blood running down his thigh from a wound. He seemed the very wrath of heaven to Darius as he cut his way forward, his blond hair streaming behind him and his face flushed red with the joy of battle. Darius' nerve shattered at the sight of the man-killing apparition coming for him. He cast away his shield, his bow, and his cloak, and leaped upon a horse, not to fight better but to flee. With him bled away the courage of the Persians as word spread of his flight, and it became clear that the phalanx had finally bested the Greek mercenaries and rolled over the bank. The center fell apart and then the right, all in a great stampede north.

Darius had the best head start of them all and did not stop until he had traveled a great distance from the battlefield. His followers were not so lucky and were slaughtered as they fled. The great butcheries of ancient battles were not in the actual fighting but in the pursuit as men were cut down from behind. As expected, the Persian cavalry suffered less than the poor infantry who died in such numbers that Ptolemy stated their bodies filled a ravine. Alexander rode into the night after Darius, until the darkness made further pursuit useless. Only then, after midnight, did he return to the camp.

Darius' royal complex had not been touched by the troops that stormed the camp. That by right was the king's spoils. When Alexander returned, he toured Darius' huge tent and marveled at its riches. Everything seemed to be made of gold. As he looked around him, he contrasted it to the relative austerity of the Macedonian court and said, "So this, it seems, is what it is to be a king."[16] His pages had taken over Darius' dinner and bath for their master. He immediately stripped off his armor for his bath, saying, "Let us wash off the sweat of battle in Darius' bath." One of his Companions remarked, "No, in Alexander's bath now. The conqueror takes over the possessions of the conquered and they should be called his."[17] He sank into the bath with great relief and later sat down to the greatest meal of his life. Just then he heard great wailing coming from a nearby royal tent. He inquired and was told these were the royal ladies and their women, who had heard that Darius' chariot and arms had been brought into the camp and believed him dead. He immediately sent to inform them that Darius had escaped and that they would not be harmed but instead shown every consideration due their rank.

The next morning Alexander accompanied by Hephestion paid a call on the royal ladies. They were met by the queen mother, Sisygambis. She prostrated herself before Hephestion who was far taller than Alexander. A eunuch gestured to Alexander as the king. Hephestion stepped back, and the queen mother realized the enormity of her unintended insult, an insult that no oriental monarch would have forgiven. She threw herself at Alexander's feet profusely apologizing. Raising her with his hand, he said with great gentleness, "Never mind, Mother. For actually he too is Alexander." It was a gallant play on the meaning of Alexander as "Protector of Men."[18]

Alexander's subsequent conduct with the royal ladies set a standard for chivalry that was to influence the ages. The Greeks thought him eccentric, but the world never forgot. He ensured that the royal ladies kept the same state they always had and showed them great honors and even doubled their establishment of servants. Their section of the camp was held off limits, protected only by the invisible wall of his honor. He treated the comely daughters of Darius as if they were his own sisters. The queen herself, who was reputed to be the great beauty of the age, he vowed to never lay eyes upon. With Sisygambis, though, he formed a deep affection such that he saw in her the gentle, loving mother he never had in Olympias. He still remained devoted to his own mother, but her demands were, as ever, insistent and painful as she raged against Antipater in letter after letter. Reading one of her letters once, he commented to Hephestion that she charged a hard rent for nine months lodging. Another time he said that one tear from her undid all of Antipater's measured arguments. In contrast, years later when Sisygambis heard that Alexander had died, she turned her face to the wall and willed herself to die of a broken heart.

Chapter 6

Son of Zeus

IN THE AFTERMATH of his victory at Issus, Alexander demonstrated a profound grasp of strategy. Curtius speaks of his rashness, but his actions at this moment were based on cool and reasoned calculation. He was thinking to a finish. Most men would have pursued Darius to Babylon directly after the battle or settled for the riches they already had won. Alexander did neither. Instead he made patience and system his allies. To have made peace would have left a still-powerful Persian Empire forever to threaten his new conquests. To have bolted after Darius with an active Persian fleet threatening his rear would have been climbing out on the proverbial limb as he penetrated deeper into Asia. The Persian fleet was a deadly encouragement to Alexander's enemies in Greece, especially Sparta and ever-trimming Athens.

He ignored the Great King who would take a long time to regain his courage and assemble a new army. He would use that time to secure his rear. That required him to destroy the Persian fleet, but his own fleet was nonexistent. Instead, he worked by one of the most elegant demonstrations of what the famous

British military theorist, B. H. Liddell Hart, would call the strategy of the indirect approach. He would deprive the Persian fleet of its bases, without which it would literally disappear. Already, he had stripped away its Aegean bases, but its main strength lay in the fleets of the cities of Phoenicia and Cyprus. The Persians relied on these maritime subjects for their ships and men. Alexander's victory poised him to descend upon Phoenicia, which he quickly did. One by one the cities submitted to him, including Sidon, which hated the Persians. Many of their kings were away with their ships in Persian service, but the victory of Issus had shaken them. In very little time, the Persian fleet simply evaporated as its component parts returned to their home cities. As he explained to his officers, once the lands surrounding the sea all the way to Egypt had been secured, "we shall be able to march on Babylon with security at home, with enhanced prestige, and with Persia excluded not only from the sea, but from the whole continent up to the Euphrates."[1]

As he accepted the submission of the first of the Phoenician cities at Marathus, opposite Sidon, an embassy from Darius arrived with a letter. He wrote that Philip and he had been friendly but that Alexander had not sought to confirm that friendship and had invaded his domains without provocation. He had only been defending himself when he met Alexander at Issus, and the fate of the battle had been decided "as some god willed; and now Darius the King asks Alexander the King to restore from captivity his wife, his mother, and his children, and is willing to make friends with him and be his ally."

Alexander rejected Darius' offer in a letter that recounted all the grievances suffered by the Greeks at the hands of the Persians for 150 years and accused Darius of Philip's murder. Then he said that if Darius wanted his family back, he should come and ask for them as a supplicant. Finally, in tones of insult so mortal that it was obviously his intention to break off negotiations, he ended:

> And in the future let any communication you wish to make with me be addressed to the King of All Asia. Do not write to me as an equal. Everything you possess is now mine; so, if you should want

anything, let me know in the proper terms, or I shall take steps to deal with you as a criminal. If, on the other hand, you wish to dispute your throne, stand and fight for it and do not run away. Wherever you may hide yourself, be sure I will seek you out.[2]

The most powerful Phoenician city was Tyre, which offered to come to terms contingent on retaining a level of independence that Alexander could not allow. He may have detected that the Tyrians were still hedging their bets on his chances. It was a position they thought they could afford; their seemingly impregnable city sat on an offshore island guarded by the single largest fleet in Phoenicia. Had they not withstood a thirteen-year siege by Nebuchadnezzar? The proximate cause of the final breach occurred when Alexander asked to sacrifice in the temple of Melkaart in Tyre, the chief deity of the Phoenicians, whom the Greeks equated with Herakles. The Tyrians refused. It was the act of defiance Alexander sought. He told them, "You think nothing of this land army because of your confidence in your position, living as you do on an island, but I am soon going to show you that you are really on the mainland. And you can be sure that I will enter your city or storm it."[3]

The Tyrians immediately sent away some of their women and children to their daughter city of Carthage far to the west. The Carthaginian ambassadors in the city urged them to resist and promised to send powerful help. The Tyrians also thought that their powerful fleet would keep open their sea lines of supply and escape. Thus, they were secure in the belief that they could stand siege. It was a challenge they should not have made to Alexander. Their submission was the lynchpin of his strategy. Their defiance would be the goad to superhuman efforts. Pushing him to outrage, the Tyrians, against all international convention, murdered the final heralds he sent and threw their bodies into the sea. The Tyrians had unsheathed the sword and thrown away the scabbard.

Alexander arrived on the scene in January 332 B.C. The mind's eye can picture him standing on the dock of the mainland city of Old Tyre looking across the water at the island fortress city of

New Tyre less than a mile away. From the threat he had already made to the Tyrians, he must have had thought through his approach long before he arrived. His personal reconnaissance confirmed it, and he set his army to work. He would cross the sea to get at New Tyre by building a mole, a solid land bridge. Old Tyre was torn down to provide the raw materials. It was an imposing task even for his finest engineers. The mole would be subject to the destructive power of a southwest wind that would serve to drive the waves against and undermine it. The wind would also ensure that catapults mounted on board ships would have unsteady platforms from which to attack the walls. The first part of the mole, across mudflats and shallow water, would be the easiest to build, but closer to Tyre the sea bottom sank precipitously. Across this deep expanse, the walls of Tyre rose 150 feet right out of the sea. His army was daunted at the task, but Alexander was already a master in improving morale. He announced that Herakles had appeared in a dream to promise victory, reminded them of the murdered heralds, and emphasized that this was the only city in their path that had not fallen. Then he had their officers tell them in no uncertain terms what was expected. The army set to work enthusiastically.

While this project was under way, he traveled with his light troops to Sidon to organize the returning Phoenician ships into a fleet that could blockade Tyre. At the same time, the work on the mole advanced steadily but tediously. Alexander found himself chaffing at this inactivity until tribesmen in the neighboring mountains of Lebanon began raiding his supply columns. Alexander was a masterful logistician, always careful of his supplies. Alexander had already written to the Jewish high priest in Jerusalem asking for supplies to feed his army. Long before Frederick or Napoleon coined the phrase, he recognized that an army marches on its stomach.

Without delay he led a punitive expedition into the mountains. His old tutor, Lysimachus, insisted on coming along despite his advancing years, saying that Phoenix was still hardy enough to accompany Achilles. As the main body pressed on, the old man began to fall behind. Alexander would not leave him as they fell farther and farther behind. As night fell, the two were alone save for only a few companions. The temperature dropped, and Lysimachus began to suffer from the cold. At the same time, they could see the watch fires of the tribesmen in the darkness all about them. Alexander disappeared into the night aiming for the nearest watch fire. He burst into the clearing and stabbed the two guards with his dagger, seized a brand from the fire, and disappeared again into the night. With the brand he built a large fire to warm the old man. The fire scared off some of the tribesman, but the bolder ones attacked only to be driven off by Alexander himself, leaving their dead and wounded behind.

During the siege, the wife of Darius died in childbirth. Alexander gave her a stately funeral befitting her rank. He was overcome with remorse at her death, regretting that he had referred to her with so little feeling in his letter to Darius and that he had lost the opportunity to be magnanimous by returning her to her husband. Her chief eunuch escaped and carried the word to Darius, who, after hearing the man out, became distraught, believing the honors of the funeral could not have been for a woman who had retained her virtue. The eunuch swore great oaths and insisted it was exactly the opposite. Darius was much moved by the nobility of his enemy and exclaimed, that if the Persians should be conquered, "grant that no other man but Alexander shall sit upon the throne of Cyrus."[4]

It had taken a while for the Tyrians to realize the seriousness of the approaching mole, but when they did they began harassing the workers with missile fire from fast boats. Alexander ordered towers and hide shields built to protect them. The Tyrians countered with a fireship that crashed into the mole and set the towers alight. Alexander ordered the mole rebuilt and that it be widened to two hundred feet to allow for greater stability and more siege equipment. Again the Tyrians were resourceful and sent divers to attach ropes to the trees layered into the mole which in turn were pulled by galleys. The head of the unstable structure again collapsed, sliding into the deep channel. By now Alexander had the adult male population of the surrounding region moving the masses of material necessary to fill the yawning deep, and the mole inched forward under a storm of missiles from the Tyrian walls. He built new towers to match the height of the wall, the highest ever built. A mass of catapults and dart throwers on the mole and in the towers returned fire, causing heavy casualties among the defenders while failing to make an impression on the massive wall itself. The mole stopped short of the wall, held at bay by the deep water. While the towers provided covering fire, ships equipped with huge rams and covered with fireproof roofs were rowed forward to break down the walls. The Tyrians threw red-hot sand at the attackers, many of whom died hideously as the grains fell inside their armor. The Tyrians used long hooks and claws to seize Macedonians and carry them over the walls or into the sea. They sent divers to cut the cables necessary to provide stability for the ram ships, but Alexander replaced them with chains. They resorted to every ingenious device known to ancient siegecraft. Great bags of soft material were lowered between the rams and the wall to cushion their blows. Whirling devices were spun along the parapets to deflect stones and missiles. In an act of frightful defiance, the Tyrians cut the throats of prisoners on the walls and threw them into the sea.

The arrival of Alexander's Phoenician fleet only gave him parity with the Tyrians. It was overwhelming superiority he needed to clamp down an effective blockage. He got that when the kings of Cyprus arrived with 120 ships to offer homage. That drove the Tyrians to even more desperate measures now that hope of relief was gone. The Carthaginians could not send the promised help; the Sicilian Greeks were burning their fields up to the walls of Carthage itself. The Tyrians made a major sortie against a squadron of the blockading force and sank a number of them but were chased back into their harbor with some loss. That was the last time they attempted an action in the water. Now Alexander realized that the assault from the mole was checked by both the last deep part of the channel and the solidity of the wall op-

posite it. He surveyed the remaining circuit of walls and identified parts there were not nearly as formidable. Against these he
directed new attacks while the battle of the mole continued un-
abated. Siege engines, catapults, and missile throwers on ships
hammered away first at the northern section of the walls, but
when that accomplished little switched to the southern walls. A
portion of the wall collapsed, and Alexander ordered a gangway
thrown across the rubble breach to make way for a reconnaissance that was repulsed. All this was done in difficult seas.

Alexander now ordered a break in the fighting to let his men
rest. Three days later, the weather had moderated, and Alexander
seized the opportunity. He encouraged his officers, "calling on
them to dare no less than he" and ordered the ship-borne catapults into action again against the south wall and brought a con-
siderable portion of it down. Ships circled the island, showering
the defenders everywhere with missiles to pin them down. Curtius relates that Alexander's "courage was great, but the danger
greater for, conspicuous in his royal insignia and flashing armour, he was the prime target of enemy missiles."[5] The catapult
ships were withdrawn as the assault force—a battalion of the
Guards and one of the phalanx—loaded in two ships, closed on
the breach. Gangways fell onto the rubble, and the Guards, led
by their commander, Admetus, charged across. Alexander was
with them and took over when Admetus was killed. He was

> neither concerned for the envy of Fortune nor fearing the menace of
> the Tyrians. Having as witness of his prowess the great army which
> had defeated the Persians, he ordered the Macedonians to follow
> him, and leading the way he slew some of those who came within
> reach with his spear, and others by a blow of his sabre. He knocked
> down still others with the rim of his shield, and put an end to the
> high confidence of the enemy.[6]

He led the Guards into the city just as his Sidonian allies
broke through the harbor and into the city as well, quickly trans-
ferring fifteen thousand panic-stricken noncombatants onto
their ships, as the fighting men of the city fought it out in the

streets and died. With the city in his hands, Alexander ordered two thousand survivors crucified. The rest of the population that had not been spirited off by their Sidonian cousins he sold into slavery. He has been criticized for this brutality, but by the standards of the time, he judged that justice did not allow for mercy. The Tyrians had repeatedly violated the rules of war and, by their desperate, last-ditch resistance, had forfeited any hope of good treatment. Alexander was perfectly prepared to be chivalrous and generous to those who surrendered, even after a hard fight, as long as the battle had been clean. He was harsh on those who broke the rules he so carefully followed. All those Tyrians who had found refuge in the temples he released. He found thirty Carthaginian ambassadors in the city, honored their protected status, and released them with a declaration of war against Carthage. Alexander concluded the seven-month siege by offering sacrifice in the temple of Melkaart just as he had promised.

As the siege ended, Alexander received another embassy from Darius who had been shamed beyond all measure at the loss of his family. He offered, in exchange for them, a great ransom of ten thousand talents, the western half of his empire, an alliance with him, and his daughter in marriage. At the council meeting, Alexander called to consider the offer, Parmenion advised, "I would take it if I were Alexander." To which Alexander replied, "And so indeed would I if I were Parmenion." He added, "[B]ut since I am Alexander, I shall send Darius a different answer."[7]

Parmenion was the spokesman for the older Macedonians; his words had great weight, and that is just what Alexander feared. Nothing would destroy the warlike spirit of the Macedonians more than negotiations that promised to buy them off handsomely. A peaceful settlement had to be ruled out at this stage. His ambitions now far exceeded the mere completion of the war of revenge authorized by the League. All Asia was within his grasp. He replied that he

> had no need . . . of Darius' money, nor was there any call upon him to accept a part of the continent in place of the whole. All Asia, including its treasure, was already his property, and if wished to marry

Darius' daughter he would do so, whether Darius liked it or not. If, moreover, Darius wanted kindliness and consideration at his hands, he must come and ask for it in person.[8]

Darius gave up all hope up of negotiation and prepared for war. Alexander would get his fight to the finish.

The strategic road to Darius led directly away from him geographically—to Egypt. Palestine fell without fighting. Barring his way to Egypt was the fortress city of Gaza some two miles inland from the sea in the midst of high sand dunes. The governor, the eunuch Batis, held the city for Darius with a garrison of Persians and Arabs and had stocked it well during the long months of the Tyrian siege. The city was built on the mound of debris left by its earlier phases and towered above the dunes. Alexander's engineers were baffled at first since the walls could not be directly approached, but Alexander ordered an earthwork built upon which his catapults could be mounted. Before the fighting began, he prepared to offer sacrifice as was his custom. A bird of prey flew over and dropped a clod upon him and then was entangled in the twisted skeins of a catapult. When Alexander asked the meaning, his seer replied that he would take the city but should take care for his safety.

Alexander heeded the warning as the artillery opened up on the walls. Batis, however, was not a passive commander, and ordered an immediate sortie of his Arab troops supported by their own catapults on the walls. The Arabs were on the point of driving the Macedonians off the earthworks when Alexander led the Guards forward to counterattack, the prophecy forgotten in the rush of excitement. He was just in time to save the position and all its artillery but was wounded severely in the shoulder by a bolt from a machine on the walls that penetrated his shield and corselet. Although the wound would be hard to heal, Alexander was delighted because it proved that the rest of the prophecy would be fulfilled.

He never thought, however, that heaven would take his assistance amiss, so he ordered all the heavy siege equipment left at Tyre brought by ship to Gaza. Then he completely encircled the city with an earthwork high enough to allow his artillery to fire directly at the walls, which were probably made largely of mud brick. The effect was dramatic as the walls began to disintegrate. They were further weakened when Alexander's men sapped through their soft rubble foundations until an entire section collapsed. A Macedonian assault secured the breach and drove the garrison from the neighboring towers. Still the defenders bravely resisted three attempts to storm through the breach. Alexander then ordered a general assault by his heavy infantry that swarmed the crumbling walls with scaling ladders.

> Once the ladders were in position, every Macedonian soldier who had any claim to courage vied with his fellows to be the first man up. The honour fell to Neoptolemus, one of the Companions; . . . hot on his heels came battalion after battalion, led by their officers, and no sooner had the leading sections penetrated the defences than they smashed down all the gates they could find and cleared an entrance for the whole army.[9]

The defenders died fighting to the last man. Their women and children were sold into slavery. It was now late fall, and the siege had taken two months. One story has Alexander taking a frightful revenge on the corpse of Batis by dragging him around the city by his heels from the back of his chariot. None of the accounts that stem from his officers who were there supports it, and it would seem completely out of character for Alexander to avenge himself on the corpse of a eunuch in a grotesque burlesque of his beloved *Iliad*.

Alexander had kicked open the gate of Egypt, and the Gift of the Nile opened its arms to him. Its Persian governor had no garrison, recognized reality, and cooperated completely. Alexander was hailed as a liberator by the Egyptians. There had been a long and friendly relationship between Egypt and Greece that freely acknowledged Egypt as the source of much of Greece's wisdom. The Egyptians had often used Greek troops to help them in the ultimately unsuccessful revolts against their Assyrian and Persian conquerors.

Alexander basked in the adulation of the Egyptians and gracefully accepted the red-and-white double crown, the *uraeus*, and the crook and flail of the pharaohs offered by the priesthoods according to their ancient rites. The Egyptians despised the Persians for their sacrileges, and Alexander's charm, tact, and genuine respect won the population over to him. He paid respect to the current sacred Apis Bull. Considering that the Persian conqueror of Egypt, Cambyses, had stabbed to death and then barbecued one of its predecessors, it was a public relations triumph. Alexander held games that attracted the most famous performers in Greece. The Macedonians would remember their stay in Egypt as an idyll. For Alexander, it may have been less demanding than the previous year, but it was no less important in his plans. He recognized the vast economic potential of Egypt, and in light of that founded just west of the Nile delta the city he named after himself that was destined to become the great entrepôt of the Mediterranean.

Egypt also held a key to his soul. The great shrine of Ammon-Ra, chief of Egypt's pantheon, equated to Zeus by the Greeks, was the most senior and respected of all shrines in the eastern Mediterranean and located at the oasis of Siwa. It was ancient when Apollo first came to Delphi. Legend surrounds the dangerous desert journey that had in the far past consumed an entire Persian army sent to loot the shrine. Alexander and his party quickly lost their way and were threatened by thirst, but rain, incredibly rare in the Western Desert of Egypt, firmed the footing and refreshed the air. Crows guided them on to the oasis itself. The stories that came out of what was surely a difficult trip did much to enhance the divine nature of Alexander's visit to the shrine itself.

The Greek-speaking high priest wished to welcome him to the shrine with a fatherly, "Oh, my son—O, paidon" in Greek, but it came out instead, "O pai Dios'—Oh, son of Zeus," or son of God. On the other hand, it would have been entirely appropriate for the priest to refer to Alexander in this way; he was pharaoh and as such was a living god to the Egyptians. Alexander asked of the god whether the murderers of his father had

Coin of Philip II, king of Macedonia and father of Alexander.
(Courtesy Library of Congress)

Olympias, the tempestuous mother of Alexander. Alexander was to say that she charged a hard rent for nine months lodging.

Demosthenes, the Athenian politician and Philip's mortal enemy.
(Courtesy Library of Congress)

The Gardens of Mieza where Aristotle taught Alexander and his young friends.
(Courtesy Jona Lendering)

Lion of Chaeronea, the monument to the Theban dead of the battle.
(Courtesy Jona Lendering)

Always a tactical innovator, Alexander ordered his men to lay under their shields as the Triballians rolled their heavy wagons down the pass at them.

(Courtesy Library of Congress)

"My son, you are invincible." Even the Priestess Apollo at Delphi
could not resist Alexander's demand for a favorable omen before he
departed on his war against Persia.
(Courtesy Library of Congress)

The first battle—Granicus. Alexander's charge up the river bank against the Persian cavalry.
(Courtesy Library of Congress)

The famous melting gaze of Alexander, caught in this bust, was magnetic in its power to win over men.
(Courtesy Library of Congress)

Alexander's speech to his officers before the battle of Issus: "You have
Alexander, they—Darius."
(Courtesy Library of Alexander)

Alexander as pharaoh. His royal name was *Meryamun Setepenre Alexandros.*
(Courtesy Jona Lendering)

The omen of Gaugamela. When the Macedonians were alarmed at an eclipse of the moon before the battle of Gaugamela, Alexander declared it a favorable omen instead—the Macedonian sun eclipsing the Persian moon. (*Courtesy Library of Congress*)

Alexander at Gaugamela, a copy in mosaic from Pompeii of a famous life painting by Philoxenus, one of the king's favorite painters.
(Courtesy Library of Congress.)

Persepolis—gate of the nations.
(Courtesy Jona Lendering)

Alexander, the Azara Herme, showed a more mature man as he campaigned in what is now Afghanistan.
(Courtesy Library of Congress)

The Rock of Aornus. Alexander led the storming of the Rock of Aornus, the mighty mountaintop fortress on the border of India. *(Courtesy Library of Congress)*

The mutiny at Opis. Alexander dealt decisively with his Macedonians when they mutinied at Opis.
(Courtesy Library of Congress)

The death of Alexander. When asked on his deathbed on what occasion he wanted his successors to remember him, he replied, "When you are happy."
(Courtesy Library of Congress)

been punished. The priest cautioned him that he was speaking of a god. Alexander then asked if any of Philip's murderers had escaped and whether he would rule all the world. The priest responded for Ammon that the overlordship of the world would be granted him and that all of Philip's assassins had been punished. Alexander made magnificent offerings to Ammon and wrote to Olympias that the god had given him secret prophecies that he would reveal to only her when next they met. Olympias' fervent stories to the child Alexander about his divine origins had sunk deep roots. Mother and son were never to meet again, and his secrets died with him.[10]

From this time, Alexander's pretensions to divine parentage become increasingly prominent. He never repudiated Philip, but apparently was able to view him as an earthly father and Zeus-Ammon as a spiritual one. Alexander rarely overlooked a practical advantage in his actions and saw that the fragrance of divinity about his name would do much to ease his way in Asia. After Egypt, his coinage would bear his likeness embellished with the horns of Ammon. It was not so uncommon a thought for the Greeks to imagine that a god had sired a son off a mortal woman. Their religion and history was full of such god-favored offspring. The Greeks also saw that exceptional excellence had a touch of divine favor to it, and was not Alexander the epitome of such excellence? What they were not prepared to accept was that the god imparted divinity with his seed to the man on earth. Alexander was aware of the difference, and was quoted frequently as saying when his red blood flowed from wounds, "What you see flowing, my friends, is blood, and not that Ichor that flows through their veins, the blessed gods."[11]

Chapter 7

"This Great Prize"

IN THE SPRING of 331 B.C., Alexander departed Egypt for his reckoning with Darius over the kingship of Asia. His army marched up the Mediterranean coast and turned east to reach the Euphrates River in August. Darius had been waiting for this moment and had lavished great care on assembling a new army. Concluding now that it had been Alexander's cavalry and not his phalanx that was the arm to be feared, he gathered from his own Iranian heartland and from the satrapies of Bactria and Sogdiana a huge and formidable cavalry force. Of quality infantry, he had very little and was probably making a virtue of necessity by relying on his cavalry. Of other infantry, he gathered hordes and upgraded their equipment. A new feature was the reintroduction of scythed chariots, vehicles with cutting blades attached to the spokes of their wheels. The chariot had long been obsolete as a serious weapon, but Darius was desperate.

A Persian observation group fled as Alexander crossed, informing Darius, in Babylon, of his approach. Initially Darius awaited him there, expecting to use the flat lands of Babylonia as the perfect ground to maneuver his host. Alexander had his own ideas, and marched along the foothills of the mountains of Armenia where the forage was greater and the heat less, ever mindful of the necessity of supplying his army and maintaining its health. The baking heat of a late Mesopotamian summer was not the battlefield he wanted. Darius, as ever surprised, marched to meet him thinking to block his passage over the Tigris. Again he was too late. Alexander crossed farther upstream, but Darius' men scorched the land ahead of them. While Alexander let his men rest after the difficult crossing, a lunar eclipse spread panic throughout the army on the night of 20/21 September. Alexander made sacrifices and received the best of all oracles—that the Macedonian sun would eclipse the Persian moon.[1] Four days later, his scouts made contact with a covering force of Persian army near a village named Gaugamela.

Alexander rode ahead and attacked the covering force with such violence that they fled. Prisoners revealed that Darius was not far off. Alexander advanced and built a fortified camp, a prudent approach in the face of the masses of Persian cavalry and the perhaps still-shaky morale of the army. After resting a few days, he again advanced and saw the huge extent of the enemy army unfolding in front of him. He called a halt to consult his officers. Parmenion advised that a careful reconnaissance of the field would be wise. The Persians might be seeding it with traps. He was probably giving a plausible explanation of thousands of Persians working on the field. Instead of placing traps, though, Darius had them smoothing the field and removing obstacles to the free maneuver and charge of his chariots.

Accompanied by his Companions and light infantry Alexander made a thorough reconnaissance of the field. At night the council met again; Parmenion suggested it would be too dangerous to meet such a force in open battle. Some trick was needed to negate their numbers, and he suggested a night attack, supported by almost everyone. Curtius captured Alexander's reaction as he fixed his eye on Parmenion.

The subterfuge you recommend to me is characteristic of brigands and thieves. For deception is their only aim. But I shall not permit Darius' absence, narrow terrain or a furtive attack at night to detract from my glory. My decision is to attack by broad daylight. I prefer to live to regret my bad luck than to be ashamed of my victory. There is also a further consideration: I have it on good authority that the Persians are posting watches and remaining under arms, so that even catching them off-guard would be impossible. So, prepare for combat!![2]

Darius indeed had kept his men at arms all night, fearing what Alexander would not lower himself to do, and thus draining away the strength and alertness of his army. Alexander's refusal to attack at night had as much to do with common sense and strategy as simple honor. Arrian points out a military fact of life that has not changed—night attacks are the most difficult to organize and carry off and the most given to mischance. As to strategy, he saw that only an open and decisive victory would break the will of the Persians to resist and bring their empire crashing down. Arrian then paraphrases the speech that must have come after this statement.

There was no need, he said, for any words from him to encourage them to do their duty; there was inspiration enough in the courage they had themselves shown in previous battles, and in the many deeds of heroism they had already performed. All he asked was that every officer of whatever rank, whether he commanded a company, a squadron, a brigade, or an infantry battalion, should urge to their utmost efforts the men entrusted to their command; for they were about to fight not, as before for Syria or Phoenicia or Egypt, but this time the issue at stake was the sovereignty of the whole Asian continent. What need, then, was there then for many words to rouse his officers to valour, when that valour was already in their own breasts? Let him but remind them each for himself to preserve discipline in the hour of danger—to advance, when called upon to do so, in utter silence; to watch the time for a hearty cheer, and, when the moment came, to roar out their battle-cry and put the fear of God into the enemy's hearts. All must obey orders promptly and pass them on without hesitation to their men; and, finally, every one of them must remember that upon the conduct of each depended the fate of all: if each man attended to his duty, success was assured; if one man neglected it, the whole army would be in peril.[3]

Thoroughly inspired, they crowded around him and begged him to have every confidence in them. He then dismissed them to bed. It had been a virtuoso leadership performance. He had dressed them down when they had taken counsel of their fears and then raised their spirits by appealing to their faith—in themselves and in him.

While Darius stayed awake with his whole army to hold his hand, Alexander slept so soundly that he was still abed long into the morning. Only he could give the order to feed the army and to put it in line of battle. As the minutes crept by, the unease grew until Parmenion took it upon himself to order the men fed. Still more time went by and no Alexander. The Persian host across the field was in line of battle, and the Macedonians could wait no more. Finally Parmenion awoke Alexander with his own hand. He apprised him of the situation and said, "What happened to your old alertness? Usually you are waking up the watch."

Alexander replied, "Do you really think I could have fallen asleep before easing my mind of the worries that that kept me from resting?"

But Parmenion, still bewildered, continued to press him after Alexander had given the signal for the army to deploy. He explained, "When Darius was burning the land, destroying villages and ruining our food supplies, I was beside myself with despair. But now that he is preparing to decide the issue in battle, what do I have to fear? Good heavens, he has answered my prayers!"[4]

When Alexander emerged from his tent, he was in such high spirits that the word ran from unit to unit, energizing the entire army. Normally, he had to be encouraged by his staff to wear his cuirass even in times of danger, but now he strode among them encased in his most magnificent array.

He wore a thickly quilted corslet which had been among the spoils captured at Issus. His helmet, the work of Theophilus, was made of steel which gleamed like polished silver, and to this was fitted a steel gorget set with precious stones. His sword . . . was a marvel of lightness and tempering, and he had trained himself to use this as his principal weapon in hand-to-hand fighting. He also wore a cloak which was more ornate than the rest of his armour . . . and this too he was in the habit of wearing in battle.[5]

He reviewed the army while riding another horse to spare Bucephalas, but when the moment came to engage, he mounted his old friend for the kill. Bucephalas would allow no man to mount him but Alexander.

The formation Alexander had devised for the army was a brilliant mix of flexibility and strength. It was designed to negate the enemy's larger numbers with a suppleness that would not break under pressure and yet would deflect much of the Persian superiority in cavalry. Its strength would lie in the coiled offensive power of the Companions and the Guard.

Alexander had already seen that Darius would command from the center as usual. Around him were his small contingents of reliable infantry that included two thousand remaining Greek mercenaries and perhaps the same number his Apple-Bearers, the remnants of his Guard. Also attached to him were a special mounted one-thousand-man contingent of Royal Kin, and the ethnic Persian cavalry. On both wings, he massed a huge cavalry superiority. The left wing, commanded by the satrap Bessus, the king's kinsman, was a mixed force, the core of which was his heavily armored Bactrians. On the right, under the command of Mazaeus, governor of Babylon, were the Medes, Parthians, Indians,[6] and Scythian Sacae nomads from beyond the empire. To the rear, Darius' valiant brother, Oxathres, commanded the huge infantry reserve. In advance of the main line, Darius had stationed his two hundred scythed chariots as well several thousand cavalry. Darius may have had as many as thirty-four thousand cavalry and fifty thousand infantry on the field. Alexander had probably more than seven thousand cavalry and almost sixteen thousand infantry in the front line, with another twelve thousand Greek allies and mercenaries in the second line.[7]

The Battle of Gaugamela
331 BC

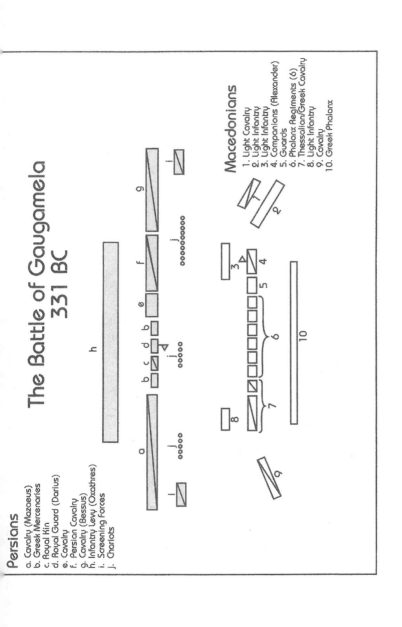

Persians

a. Cavalry (Mazaeus)
b. Greek Mercenaries
c. Royal Kin
d. Royal Guard (Darius)
e. Cavalry
f. Persian Cavalry
g. Cavalry (Bessus)
h. Infantry Levy (Oxathres)
i. Screening Forces
j. Chariots

Macedonians

1. Light Cavalry
2. Light Infantry
3. Light Infantry
4. Companions (Alexander)
5. Guards
6. Phalanx Regiments (6)
7. Thessalian/Greek Cavalry
8. Light Infantry
9. Cavalry
10. Greek Phalanx

Alexander correctly discounted the infantry and concentrated on dealing with the cavalry. He did this by refusing each wing or pulling it back in a stepped or bended shape, making envelopment much more difficult. On the refused wings, he placed cavalry, mercenaries, and light troops. On the right, he advanced various cavalry and light units as well. On his main line, he commanded the right made up of his companions and the Agrianes. To the left next were the Guards, then the six battalions of the phalanx, allied cavalry, and the Thessalian cavalry. The second line had the orders to turn front to back should the main line be enveloped. It was a wonderfully flexible defensive disposition for a very offensively minded commander. However, its defensive nature was meant to give its offensive arm, the Companion Cavalry led by Alexander himself, the opportunity to seize the main chance when it should appear.

The first move was Alexander's. He kept extending his refused right flank, which caused Bessus to extend his line to the left. Alexander was drawing Bessus' excellent cavalry away from the center before an arrow had been shot. He was also moving toward the edge of the area that had been so laboriously cleared for the Persian chariots. Getting increasingly nervous, Darius ordered Bessus to envelop Alexander's right. The attempt was disrupted by the cavalry formations Alexander had placed in advance of his refused flank. Alexander kept feeding in more formations and drove back the first wave. Bessus committed more and more of his Bactrians until a major cavalry battle had developed.

Darius now committed his chariots, which initially caused serious casualties but were quickly shot up by the light infantry Alexander had placed in front of his right. A few got through and headed for his infantry in the main line, but the excellence of their drill allowed them to open ranks and let the careening vehicles through. Now trapped behind the main line and the mercenary reserve, they were brought down by the royal grooms.

Things were going less well on Alexander's left where Parmenion's Thessalians were in the fight of their lives against odds of five to one or more. In the center the phalanx closed with

Oxathres' infantry, which Darius had ordered forward. Darius may also have led the Royal Kin and the Apple-Bearers into the fight himself. At this moment, the battle hung in the balance. Mazaeus was pressing hard with the Persian right, the center was closely engaged, and the left was confused. Darius was demonstrating more active leadership than at Issus, and it was still anyone's battle. At this point, Darius saw that the tide had turned against his cavalry on his left wing and threw in his Persian cavalry. Alexander instantly saw his chance as the Persian center was uncovered by the departure of these troops. Into this gap he charged, with his Companions and the Guards shouting the Macedonian war cry. It was the decisive moment of the battle.

Darius at first withstood the shock of the attack, throwing javelins from his chariot and urging on his Royal Kin and the Apple-Bearers. The two kings were now within killing distance, and Alexander threw a javelin at Darius. He missed Darius but killed his driver who was thrown out of the chariot by the impact. A cry of alarm went up from the surrounding Persians. Those men farther away took it to mean that the Great King had been struck down. These were the first to panic and run. Truly, Homer in the *Iliad* sang, "Godsent Panic seized them, comrade of bloodcurdling Rout."[8] The Persian center unraveled from the outside in. As his own Guards disappeared around him, Darius withdrew his chariot into the blinding dust raised by so many men and horses.

At the same time, things went from bad to worse for Parmenion on the left wing. Mazaeus' assault was both enveloping his flank and fixing his front, forcing the two phalanx battalions on the left to stand fast in his support instead of moving forward with the others. A gap opened and Parthian and Indian cavalry dashed through. A number of them rode on and burst upon the surprised Macedonian camp. When they tried to rescue Darius' family, Sisygambis sat immobile in her chair and refused to go "since she neither trusted the uncertain turns of fortune nor would sully her gratitude to Alexander."[9]

Mazaeus' skillful handling of his wing was on the point of

yielding him a victory when Parmenion sent to Alexander for help. It was a miracle that the messenger found him in the confusion and dust, but Alexander turned the Companions about to Parmenion's aid. Before he could reach the fight, Alexander's Greek mercenaries stationed behind the phalanx attacked the Parthian and Indian cavalry that had not gone off to the camp and also threw their weight into stopping the envelopment. Alexander's forethought was paying off. At the same time, news of Darius' flight and Alexander's imminent arrival swept through Mazaeus' ranks. Parmenion instantly sensed the change, urged the Thessalians on, and they surged forward. Before Parmenion's eyes, the enemy disengaged and fled. In this moment of victory, the Companions also fought their dearest fight. They were in the path of these masses of cavalry attempting to escape and made desperate by their fear.

> The ensuing struggle was the fiercest of the whole action; one after another the Persian squadrons wheeled in file to the charge; breast to breast they hurled themselves on the enemy. Conventional cavalry tactics—manoeuvring, javelin throwing—were forgotten; it was every man for himself, struggling to break through as if in that alone laid his hope of life. Desperately and without quarter, blows were given and received, each man fighting for mere survival without any further thought of victory or defeat. About sixty of Alexander's Companions were killed. . . .[10]

The general pursuit now began, and the slaughter was worse than at Issus, mostly among the fleeing infantry though most of the cavalry got away. The prisoners, though, far exceeded the killed. Parmenion overran the Persian camp as Alexander rode on to storm the Persian base at Arbela, only to find Darius long gone. For the second time, Darius had left behind his chariot and weapons as he had mounted a fast horse. The accounts of the casualties cannot be trusted, listing only one hundred Macedonian dead, but the item of one thousand dead horses, half among the Companions, might give a closer hint of the losses. In any case, whatever the cost, it had been worth it to Alexander. Darius had been broken, leaving the sovereignty of Asia in the dust of the battlefield. Alexander, to paraphrase Napoleon, picked it up with the tip of his sword.

Darius was now of no matter as Alexander moved to secure the prize. He moved directly south on Babylon and approached the city in battle array, only to be met by Mazaeus who surrendered the city and its treasury. The population received him as a liberator, and Alexander did much to encourage this good will by honoring the Babylonian gods long insulted by the Persians. Alexander wisely paid the troops with the money and gave them a month's leave in the greatest fleshpot in the world. The release of all that money into the pockets of the Babylonians also did much to foster good will. For the first time he appointed a Persian as satrap, the gallant Mazaeus himself.

After rousing the army from its pleasure with games and exercises, he marched on Susa, the Persian's administrative capital. Its governor opened the gates and its treasury vaults of fifty thousand silver talents. Alexander also found there the treasures Xerxes had looted from Greece 150 years before, including the twin bronze statues of the tyrannicides, Harmodius and Aristogeiton, hauled away from burned Athens. These he returned to the Athenians who set them up on the way to the Acropolis, where Arrian saw them almost five hundred years later. In Susa, Alexander was joined by fifteen thousand replacements from Macedonia. The cavalry he assigned to the Companions to fill the empty ranks, and the others he distributed to their ethnic units. He took the opportunity to make promotions based on merit among his commanders and not by their traditional tribal affiliations.

His next objective was the Persis, the Persian heartland, and Persepolis its great ceremonial capital. Its way was barred by a mountain tribe that demanded of him the same tribute the Persian kings had paid for passage. Alexander changed that arrangement. He found a way around through their mountains, fell upon them with slaughter, and left them burdened with an enormous annual tribute of livestock. Alexander now divided the army, sending Parmenion the long-but-easy way with most of the troops. He took the harder but quicker route with the Companions, the Guards, the phalanx, and the Agrianes. At the narrow pass called the Persian Gates, he found Ariobarzanes, the local satrap, with a force larger than his own strung across the way. In a rare act of misjudgment, Alexander attempted to bounce the fortified pass but was repulsed with heavy losses as the Persians rained boulders and missiles from above into the Macedonians. He pulled back with his dead still in the pass, a bitter lesson. Leaving Craterus with two regiments of the phalanx and a few archers, he left at night on a track through the snowy mountains with a local guide. The force left behind was to attack the pass when Alexander's trumpets announced he had descended into the Persian rear. After a twelve-mile march, Alexander divided his force again. Keeping the Guards, one regiment of the phalanx, archers, Agrianes, and the Royal Squadron of the Companions with him. The rest he sent farther behind the pass to seize the vital river crossing to Persepolis. With his picked force, he overran three outposts before dawn and burst into the Persian camp, which was caught completely unawares. The trumpet sounded, and Craterus' men burst through the pass. The Persians were cut to pieces, and only a few escaped. Alexander lost no time but marched quickly on Persepolis, crossed the newly bridged river, and raced for the city.

On the outskirts, he met a horrific sight. About eight hundred aged Greeks had come as supplicants. They had been craftsmen and artisans carried off by Persian kings who had amputated hands and feet, noses and ears—those parts not needed for their skills. Alexander burst into tears at the sight as outrage and pity spread through the army. He received their leaders with respect and offered to return them to their homes, but they could not bear the shame and pity of their mutilations and asked to remain where they were. He endowed them richly and exempted them from taxation.

As he entered, he gave over the city to a brutal sack, the memory of the supplicants fresh in everyone's mind. It was handsome reward for all their sufferings and exertions, for the city was filled with great mansions and the wealth of the empire's elite. His men fell upon the city in an orgy of destruction and murder until Alexander intervened and ordered that the women not be harmed nor stripped of their clothes and jewelry. He himself went straight for the palace, having entered Persepolis before its garrison could loot the great treasury: the accumulated hording of three hundred years of empire, which yielded a stunning 120,000 talents in gold and silver. Alexander had it all removed. He had other plans for this heart city of the Persian Empire. His willingness to give it over to rapine also indicated that the city had no future in his empire.

What came later proved that. Alexander had told his army that Persepolis was the most hateful city in Asia, from which the Persians had launched their unholy wars upon Greece. Its imperial splendor was its world-famous palace, its great hall supported by one hundred enormous columns that rose to a great height, and its staircases lined with bas-reliefs of the Apple-Bearers. He burned it. Historians have argued the reason ever since. Arrian contends it was an act of policy, the final revenge of Greece. Parmenion was said to have argued against it. The other tradition is the more lurid and says that the decision to fire the palace was made at a drunken feast. The inspiration was the courtesan Thais, who suggested the act as revenge for the burning of her native Athens by Xerxes. His companions roared their approval, and Alexander, drunk by now as well, led the band of revelers inside, letting Thais and the women begin throwing torches into the building and setting the draperies alight until the fires licked up the walls and set afire the great cedar beams of the ceiling in the hall of columns. Thais exulted that it was the hand of a woman that brought down the palace of the mighty Persian kings. Apparently, when his head cleared, Alexander regretted his arson. If this story is true, it is easy to understand that at a moment of complete release lubricated by wine, enticed by one of the most beautiful women of the age, and riding the emotional high of his roaring companions, Alexander lost his grip and did this thing so unworthy of himself.

This act betrayed no hostility to the Persians, only to their sovereignty. He had shown a special reverence to Cyrus, the founder of that empire, at his tomb at Pasagardae. Because of Alexander's mildness, the rest of Persis submitted quickly, and all that was now left to Alexander was to hunt down Darius who had taken refuge at the Persian summer capital of Ecbatana in northeastern Iran. The news of Alexander's pursuit drove Darius to the east. He had retained a small army of Persians and Bactrians under Bessus, as well as a few thousand of the ever-faithful Greek mercenaries. Many of Darius' followers, particularly Bessus, had lost all respect for him and saw him as an obstacle to resistance. They thought to either ingratiate themselves by handing Darius over to Alexander or to kill him and resume the war from the stronghold of Bactria with Bessus as the new Great King. The mercenary commander tried to warn Darius and urged him to place himself under the protection of the Greeks. But Darius was a broken man, unable to take positive action even when disaster threatened. Bessus seized Darius, put him in chains, threw him into a cart, and set off for Bactria.

As soon as he learned Darius had left Ecbatana, Alexander went in swift pursuit, actively gathering intelligence of his location, learning that Darius was in danger from his own followers. He gathered his generals and said, "The task that remains is of great importance but the effort will be brief. Darius is not far off, deserted by his troops or overthrown by them. In his person lies our victory, and speed will reward us with this great prize."[11]

His pursuit was relentless. He shed more and more men who could not keep up in the July heat until he retained only a few hundred cavalry. Alexander took the surrender of a number of Persian lords who had deserted rather than serve Bessus. One gladly pointed out a short cut. Curtius writes, "Alexander was ever the man of action, but the deserter now fired him up with an obsessive desire to catch Bessus." The latter had grown careless and kept his army in poor control. When Alexander finally caught up with the straggling, dispirited force, he fell upon them like a thunderbolt. At his approach, they broke. Although they heavily outnumbered the Macedonians, "Alexander's name and reputation, extremely important factors in warfare, turned them into panic-stricken flight."[12]

Panic overcame Bessus as well, and he ordered Darius killed. He was speared and left for dead, his servants killed, and his mules maimed. The pain- and thirst-tormented animals carried him off the road to a spring. There he was found by a Macedonian soldier, Polystratus, who was seeking the water as well. The man filled his helmet to ease Darius' misery with a drink. Darius knew death was upon him and was anxious to clear his soul. He charged Polystratus to relate to Alexander his last words: that he died indebted to Alexander for the treatment of his family, which revealed his noble spirit, that he had been more fortunate in his enemies than in his kinsmen (Bessus), and that his prayers were all he could offer Alexander—prayers that he achieve dominion over the world. He then asked that Alexander avenge him, not for his own death, but to uphold the sanctity of kingship. He grasped Polystratus' hand and died.

Alexander was summoned and heard Polystratus out. He threw his cloak over the dead man and wept at the cruelty of fate that had dragged him so low. He treated his body in royal fashion and sent it to Sisygamibis at Persepolis for a royal burial with the other Persian kings.

Chapter 8

Macedonians with Wings

With Darius dead, the war of revenge was finished. Alexander dismissed the Corinthian League troops with a handsome bonus. Those who wished, reenlisted with his army. It was a dangerous act but a more important statement. From now on, he would be acting on his own authority as King of Asia. The dangerous part was the precedent of demobilization. It was not only the Greeks from the League, but the Macedonians who wanted to go home. The rumor started, as camp rumors do, with the wish father to the thought, that the king had given permission for them to depart as well, and instantly the camp became a turmoil of happy, packing men. This greatly distressed Alexander, who had already planned to campaign as far as India. He gathered his officers who vied to support him, but begged that he personally address the men.

He convened an assembly and reminded them that their work was not finished. Should they leave now, the peoples they had conquered would rise, led by Bessus who had now styled him Darius' successor: "The moment they see our backs turned they will be after us. . . . So we must either let go what we have taken or seize what we do not yet hold." He ended with an appeal to chivalrous justice. "It is a noble undertaking, I can tell you, one that will be counted among your most glorious achievements—that you avenged even your enemy Darius, letting your hostility towards him end with his death, by executing his murderer, and that you allowed no criminal to slip through your fingers."[1]

Alexander had called in a lover's due, and won. The bond between Alexander and his army was perhaps the greatest love affair of history. His men in the ranks would deny him nothing. Among some of his senior officers, there was less enthusiasm. Alexander's imperial transformation was bad enough for the senior Macedonians, more used to the first-among-equals nature of their kingship. What made it worse was his adoption of a number of Persian court customs and items of dress. He was lowering himself to the level of a conquered race, an enormous affront to the race-conscious Macedonians. Being blunt men, they did not see the value of enlisting the active support of the conquered with the simple respect inherent in Alexander's actions. The younger men were more eager to follow his example.

Alexander's first action on the campaign was to get the army back into shape. It now trailed an immense train of baggage belonging to the troops as well as the generals. He stopped the train, had the animals led away, and set fire to his own baggage. Everyone followed suit, though they had rescued much of their belonging from burning cities in the first place. "Presently common sense eased their chagrin. Fit for service and ready for anything, they were pleased that they had sacrificed their baggage and not their discipline."[2]

Alexander planned to invade Bactria directly from northeastern Iran but was diverted by a threat to his communications. Satibarzanes, the satrap of Areia in western Afghanistan, whom he had recently confirmed in his office, had murdered his Macedonian adviser and risen in revolt to support Bessus. Taking his cavalry and light troops, Alexander made a forced march and so disconcerted Satibarzanes that he fled to Bessus, leaving his people on a fortified mountain to withstand Alexander. The king felt a hot dry wind blowing toward it and ordered its forests set on fire. The wind-fed conflagration consumed the rebels. Rebels—those who raised arms to Alexander were now rebels. He was no longer just pursuing a regicide. The rebellion had given him pause, though. Rather than rushing after Bessus, he subdued two other satrapies, Drangiana in southwestern Afghanistan and Arachosia (around Kandahar) in the southeast to secure his communications.

It was during this pause that a plot to murder Alexander was discovered that implicated the commander of his own Guards, Philotas, son of Parmenion. Even his bodyguard was implicated. The mutterings against the king's ambitions and oriental habits had festered and had been revealed by an ordinary soldier. Alexander had been careless of his own person, accessible to a large number of people. His trust in his friends was childlike in its absolute nature. He must have been stunned when the news was brought but acted with typical dispatch. Alexander had the legacy of too many murdered Macedonian kings, himself a witness to his father's, to be squeamish. The conspirators, including Philotas, were condemned by the army in assembly and executed. That left Parmenion, who commanded Alexander's line of communications, as a danger; the death of his son set in train a blood feud that overrode any other loyalty. Swift-racing dromedaries carried agents to his headquarters with orders for Parmenion's generals to kill him. Alexander had served notice he would crush any opposition. He also reshuffled major commands. No single man would have Parmenion's power. Large commands were subdivided. The Companions were split into two commands given to Cleitus and Hephestion, one a member of the old guard and one of the younger generation. Ptolemy became his personal bodyguard.

Alexander wintered in the rich farmlands around modern Helmand while Bessus sent Satibarzanes back to Areia to stir up revolt. This time Alexander did not go, but dispatched his boyhood friend, Erigyius, who killed Satibarzanes with his own hand. Alexander founded Alexandria in Arachosia (Kandahar) in the first months of 329 B.C. and then marched north to invade

Bactria centered on the Kabul valley. There he founded another city, Alexandria in Caucaso (Bagram) and waited for the snows to melt before he could march further. Bessus had devastated the land in front of Alexander, an act of desperation deepened by the failure to hold the loyalty of the Bactrians who deserted in droves. Finally, Bessus abandoned Bactria, crossing the Oxus River (Amu Darya) into Sogdiana, and joined forces with the Sacae, in the hope of fighting a guerrilla war.

When the snows melted enough for passage, Alexander led his army through one of the passes to the north to seize Drapsaca (Kunduz) and hurried north across seventy-five miles of waterless desert, a journey more severe than any battle the army had faced. When two scouts returned from the river with water skins, they offered a cup first to Alexander, who took it. Before drinking he asked for whom it was intended. When they said it was for their children, he returned it full. "I cannot bear to drink alone and it is not possible for me to share so little with everybody. Go quickly and give your sons what you have brought on their account."[3] The army was straggling badly, but Alexander had those who were first to arrive drink, then fill skins and return to help their struggling comrades. At dusk he set fires on the hills to guide those who had wandered away. Many were so crazed by thirst that they overdrank and died from shock.

The army crossed on floats made from tents stuffed with dried grass. Bessus' failures and Alexander's relentless pursuit were too much for Besus' followers, and he was now betrayed by his chief supporter, the Sogdian satrap, Spitamenes. Stripped naked and scourged, Besus was dragged before Alexander, who asked him why he had killed his lawful lord. "What bestial madness possessed you that you should dare to imprison and then murder a king from whom you had received exemplary treatment? Yes, and you rewarded yourself for this treachery with the title of king which was not yours."[4] Bessus said it was to ingratiate himself with the conqueror, exactly the wrong approach to take with Alexander. He sent Bessus back to Persia to be tried by Persian custom at the hands of Darius' brother, Oxathres, who cut off his nose and ears and impaled him slowly on a sharpened stake. Alexander was astute in the choice of Oxathres. By allowing the man to fulfill his blood feud with the murderer of his brother, Alexander bound to him this Persian royal, renowned for valor.

Alexander paused long enough to scour the country for horses to replace the severe losses from crossing the mountains and desert; he was wounded by an arrow in the fibula when he led an attack on tribesmen who had ambushed a foraging party. Who was to carry his litter provoked an acrimonious argument between the infantry and the cavalry. The Companions said that since the king rode into battle with them, it was their due. The infantry replied that it was their duty to carry the wounded, and now when the wounded man was the king, the cavalry were trying to steal the honor. In the end, Alexander had to play Solomon and order them to take turns as the army marched to Maracanda (Samarkand). It then moved north to the Jaxartes River (Syr Darya), which formed the border of the Persian Empire; he confirmed it as his own. On the other side were only nomadic barbarians. On the river he founded another city, Alexandria Eschate—Alexandria the Furthest (Khodzhent/ Leninabad). There he learned that Spitamenes had raised both Bactria and Sogdiana in revolt behind him. These events were to usher in the most arduous campaign of his life.

Alexander's immediate problem was to reduce the seven towns along the river that had gone over to the rebels. Their mud-brick walls were no match for the ferocity of a Macedonian assault, and they fell in quick succession. The rules of war of that period were clear for any city that resisted to the last—the males were slaughtered and the women and children sold into slavery. One of the towns was named Cyropolis, built by Cyrus the Great. For that reason and also surely because it was the strongest, he wanted to spare the city, but the defenders determined to resist. Alexander intended to batter his way through but noticed that a dry riverbed ran under the walls through several channels, each below the base of the wall. It was just enough space for a man to crawl through. Alexander himself led a small party under the wall, crept to a gate, and opened it to admit the army. The parallels to the Trojan Horse must have been irresistible to him.

Another town had offered to surrender too, but instead murdered the fifty cavalrymen he had sent as emissaries. In a rage, Alexander stormed the town that now offered the stoutest resistance of any of the doomed seven. As he led the assault, he was struck by a stone in the head and throat and sank into the darkness of a severe concussion. His army thought the wound mortal, but his incredible powers of endurance roused him, though he seems to have suffered both vocal and visual impairment for a while. He did not allow that to slacken the pace of the siege but intensified it, "his anger spurring on his instinctive speed of action." His engineers tunneled under the walls, bringing down a large section through which the army stormed.

As the ashes of the seven towns smoldered, Alexander learned that Spitamenes had besieged the Macedonian garrison of Maracanda and sent a force of about three thousand men to its relief. At the same time, a large number of Scythian Sacae arrived across the river to join in the war. While he watched them daily taunt him from across the river and send arrows flying his way, he learned that Spitamenes had ambushed and wiped out most of the relief force. Confronted front to back with emergencies, Alexander revealed again his mastery of the art of war. He immediately suppressed the news of the defeat at Maracanda. That could not last long, so he moved quickly and gathered his officers around him so they could hear his reasoning. He was yet not fully recovered from his wounds; bone splinters continued to work themselves out of his leg, and his voice could barely be heard. He had less fear of the Scythians, he said, than of their timing with Bactria still in revolt. To do nothing would embolden them further and bring greater numbers to endanger the army's rear.

But suppose we cross the Tanais (Jaxartes) and with a bloody slaughter of the Scythians demonstrate that we are universally invincible? . . . Mind you, the slightest hesitation on our part and the

Scythians will be on our backs. Are we alone in being able to swim rivers? Many things that until now have given us victory will recoil upon us. Fortune teaches the arts of war to the defeated as well as the victors. . . . So by avoiding war we shall strengthen them, and instead of launching an attack we shall have to be on the defensive. The logic of my strategy is clear. But because I have not ridden a horse or done any marching since receiving this wound, I doubt if the Macedonians will let me execute my plan. Yet if you are ready to follow me, my friends, I am well. I have strength enough to meet the demands of the operation. Alternately, if my life's end is already at hand, in what exploit could I achieve a finer death?[5]

His seer, however, said it was inauspicious. Alexander replied that "it was better to face the worst of perils than for the conqueror of nearly all Asia to make himself ridiculous to a pack of Scythians."[6] He crossed the river and, by means of a decoy formation, put the Scythians in a trap that he closed with a mass charge of his cavalry and light troops, killing fifteen hundred of them. The heat that day was so great, though, that Alexander came down with severe dysentery after drinking polluted water and had to be carried back to the camp. That saved the Sacae from further loss, but their king quickly offered submission. Rousing himself from his sickbed, Alexander then rushed south with a picked force to raise the siege of Maracanda, crossing the almost 160 miles in three days and nights. As he drew near on the morning of the fourth day, Spitamenes fled ahead of him. Alexander paused to give decent burial to his men, and then ravaged the surrounding region for supporting Spitamenes. The worst of the winter was spent in Bactria until reinforcements and supplies reached the army, which he transferred to Maracanda. Alexander had had his first taste of guerrilla war and quickly learned to master it. He laced Sogdiana with strong garrisons, then scorched Spitamenes' recruiting grounds. The Sogdian baron had been his most capable opponent, but, bit by bit, Alexander strangled his resources.

Lost in his plans, Alexander failed again to see growing dissatisfaction among his men with his increasing "orientalizing."

He had made a severe misjudgment when he tried to introduce his court to the Persian custom of prostration, or *proskynesis,* before the king. The Macedonians and Greeks were outraged. A man prostrated himself before the gods, not men, nor men who took on the airs of gods, son of Zeus-Ammon or not.[7] Another factor was also acting as an irritant—Alexander's endless recounting of his own deeds. No one contested their accuracy, only that they seemed to exclude the rest of the army as having had anything to do with his glories. Alexander was not the only one who valued renown above all. Events now rapidly spun out of control at a late night drinking party, a feast day for Dionysios, his mother's god. Alexander had unaccountably sacrificed instead to Castor and Pollux. Wine freed his good sense as he began boasting of his own accomplishments and belittling Philip's, egged on by the sycophants among his generation. That was too much for the also-drunk Cleitus. He spoke his mind now, defending Philip and the older Macedonians. He reminded Alexander of having saved his life at Granicus. Waving his right arm, he said, "This is the hand that saved you, Alexander, on that day!"

Incensed, Alexander grabbed a spear and tried to kill him but was held back by his friends as Ptolemy dragged Cleitus outside. Alexander raged, "What? Have I nothing left of royalty but the name? Am I to be like Darius, dragged in chains by Bessus and his cronies?"

Cleitus was in an equal rage and returned, shouting, "Here I am, Alexander!" The king seized another spear before anyone could intervene and ran Cleitus through. He stood there over the dead man as the enormity of his act sank in. The scene stunned the room into silence. Alexander pulled out the spear and turned it upon himself as his guards sprang forward and wrested it with difficulty from him. He wailed to his absent adored nurse, Cleitus' sister, Lanike. "Ah, a good return I have made you for your care, now I am a man! You have lived to see your sons die fighting for me, and now with my own hand I have killed your brother."[8] Mary Renault wrote:

No judgment on it has been harsher than Alexander's own. He had killed Parmenion as a king, responsibly. This time he had killed as a man, who could not hold his drink or his temper. As a king, he had illegally killed a Macedonian asserting his right of free speech. As a Greek he had killed a benefactor and a guest; aspects whose enormity we can scarcely assess now. His shame was proportioned to his pride; for a time he found himself intolerable.[9]

The shock and self-loathing triggered a fall into near madness as he cried and screamed through the night. The next day he had the blood-soaked body brought to him and tried to speak to it until his friends removed it. He shut himself up for three days, refusing to eat or drink. Realizing he was willing himself to die, his friends burst into his tent and pleaded with him to come around. The army had spontaneously held an assembly and declared Cleitus a traitor and Alexander's act lawful. They would have denied him a decent burial but Alexander ordered it. The next ten days were spent bringing him back from the edge of the abyss. The priest of Dionysios had the most persuasive argument. Alexander had slighted the god who had chosen the weapon of madness in the wine, Dionysios' talisman. For this genuinely religious king, it brought a thin balm—the god had made him do it. He never truly believed it but clutched at it like a drowning man seizing anything that floats by in a storm.

Action brought a form of oblivion as well, despite the midwinter weather, and Alexander marched east along the Oxus, stamping out rebellion. Leaving Craterus, one of his best phalanx commanders,[10] to command the forces garrisoning Bactria, he crossed the Oxus to march into eastern Sogdiana, where barons continued to hold out in their mountain fortresses. Winter was a more dangerous enemy. The army was struck by an ice storm as it passed through a mountain forest, plunging the temperature below zero. The army staggered about as men and animals dropped out to huddle under trees and slip into hypothermia. Men froze to death in such lifelike poses that they seemed to be talking to each other. It was in such moments of catastrophe that Alexander showed his greatness as a leader. He kept the men moving, got them to fell trees and build great bonfires, to search out the native dwellings and crowd into them. He was everywhere, imparting his energy to fight the paralysis of the cold. He found one Macedonian soldier shambling into the camp from the storm, dazed and near death, and put him into his own chair by the fire, saying, "Now do you see how much better a time you have of it under a king than the Persians do? With them, to have sat in the king's seat would have been a capital offense—but in your case it proved a life-saver."[11] Perhaps he was still feeling the sting of those who accused him of becoming an oriental tyrant. The army came through but at the cost of two thousand soldiers, servants, and camp followers.

His first objective was the baronial fortress known as the Sogdian Rock. Its sheer cliff walls offered no way to the top save a narrow, easily defended trail. The master of the stronghold, Oxyathres, was not present, but his castellan had all the arrogance of the great man and taunted Alexander's call for his surrender, saying that only if the Macedonians had wings would they be able to take the rock. That was just not the sort of challenge to throw at Alexander, and he said that he would, indeed, show these barbarians that Macedonians could fly. He called for volunteers among his men with mountain-climbing experience, and chose three hundred, reminding them of their deeds and their faith in each other. He concluded:

> Nature has set nothing so high that it cannot be surmounted by courage. . . . Get to the top. When you have reached it, give me a signal with pieces of white cloth and I shall advance troops to divert the enemy's attention from you to us. The first man to reach the summit shall have a reward of ten talents; the man behind him will receive one less and so on up to ten men. But I am sure that my wishes are of more concern to you than my generosity.[12]

The men were eager. They used iron tent pegs as pitons and strong flaxen ropes to work their way up the mountain face. Thirty fell to their deaths in the deep snow banks below, but the rest made it to the top and waited the night hidden from the defenders. In the morning Alexander saw their linen flags and raised the camp to a great clamor. When the defenders looked down, Alexander pointed up to his Macedonians perched on the ledge above them. Their morale flattened, they surrendered.

Among the captives were the women folk of Oxyathres. Oxyathres quickly presented himself to Alexander when he heard of their good treatment and, in appreciation, offered them to dance for Alexander. Alexander was so overwhelmed with the classic dark-haired beauty of the baron's daughter, Roxane, that he fell head-over-heels in love for the first time in his life. He precipitously asked for her hand, though he could have simply taken her by force. The army may have grumbled a bit at a foreign wife, but Philip had taken many campaign wives to secure provinces and tribes. For Alexander, it was a politic move to help cement the allegiance of the two obdurate provinces that had consumed two years of hard fighting. In the meantime, Spitamenes had been giving Craterus a difficult time, but Alexander's deputy was as inexorable as his king, and eventually drove him into the desert, where he was murdered by his own Scythian allies. Craterus' success now marked him as Alexander's second-in-command.

Alexander's name alone was now enough to bring submission. At the same time, those nearest Alexander, a half-dozen of the royal pages, were plotting to kill him. Chief among them was Hermolaus whom Alexander had personally flogged for an act of *lèse majesté*. On a royal hunt, Hermolaus had grossly insulted the king by killing the boar Alexander had picked out for his own. The young man had complained to the royal historian and their teacher, Callisthenes, the nephew of Aristotle. Callisthenes recounted the heroism of the two Athenian tyrannicides and may have done more to encourage Hermolaus to suborn other pages to help murder the king during their watch. Callisthenes was already blatantly disaffected and suicidally indiscreet; he had publicly insulted Alexander over the *proskynesis* issue. That night, Alexander partied late into the morning. One of the pages lost his nerve the next day and revealed the plot. The king pardoned him and arrested the others. Callisthenes' arrest followed. The assembly of the army stoned the pages to death, and Alexander hanged Callisthenes. The intellectuals of Athens never forgave him for the execution of their fellow philosopher and assailed his memory for centuries.

Chapter 9

India

After two years of hard campaigning, the vast area between Persia and India had been subdued. For Alexander, it had not been an end in itself, but the necessary jumping off point for his growing yearning, his *pothos*, to march over the mountains to fabled India. He would outdo the Persians, who had only briefly held western India; he would find the encircling sea and the limits of the earth. He would also outdo his mother's patron god, Dionysios, who, legend had it, had traveled to the west from India. Herakles had conquered this way as well.

In the spring of 327 B.C., Alexander was ready. Already Indian princes had been paying court, providing intelligence, and offering submission as a way to deal with the inevitable, as well as to secure Alexander as an ally against their local enemies. Chief among them was Omphis of Taxila. Alexander concentrated his army at Alexandria in Caucaso, giving part to Hephestion and Perdiccas with orders to march through the lowlands along the Kabul River valley. A new addition to his force was a large contingent of Scythian horse archers. He took his picked units and subdued the kingdoms north of the main force. Many submitted or simply abandoned their cities and fled in his path. The recalcitrant were stormed by the usual combination of Macedonian ingenuity and siege technology. The kingdom of the Assaceni in the valley of the Lower Swat offered the most determined resistance by dispersing most of their army to their fortresses and cities. They were stormed one by one. The most impregnable was the mountain fortress of Aornus, which rose eight thousand feet above sea level. Legend had it that Herakles had tried but failed to storm it, an irresistible challenge for Alexander. The king personally led the attack that secured the saddle below the fortress. From that position, his engineers built a massive mound from which catapults tormented the defenders. Under the ploy of negotiations, they tried to escape, but Alexander was informed and stormed the fortress with his Agrianes and phalanx troops as the Assaceni were leaving, slaughtering many.

The army crossed the Indus in the spring of 326 B.C. after holding games and sacrifices. On the other side, they were in the friendly territory of Taxila and lavishly supplied as Alexander entered the capital twenty miles north of modern Islamabad. Omphis was only too glad to point out his hostile neighbor, Porus, whose kingdom lay beyond the Hydaspes (Jhelum) River to the east. Porus defiantly refused even token submission, and Alexander marched. He found Porus and his army on the other side of the substantial Hydaspes, an obstacle the Indian king had no intention of letting Alexander cross. Already the melting snows of the Himalayas had begun to swell its current, and the monsoons would be on them in June. All Porus had to do was wait and watch. He commanded an excellent Indian army as well, though smaller than Alexander's. His thirty thousand infantry, mostly archers, made up the bulk of his force, but its offensive arms were its 4,000 cavalry, 180 chariots, and 85 elephants. Porus strongly guarded every ferry and possible crossing point with his elephants, which would make a cavalry landing from barges impossible.[1]

Alexander camped on the river in May and immediately set about confusing Porus as to his intentions by giving strong indications that he would wait for the monsoons to pass. Endless convoys of grain provided by Omphis filled his camp. At the same time, Alexander further confused Porus by making daily feints up and down the river with strong and very noisy forces as if he intended to cross. Porus took the bait and followed these detachments on his side of the river. Day after day, this game went on, until Porus grew tired of it as mere bravado. By this time, a large number of boats and small ships from the Indus arrived overland in sections, were reassembled, and immediately controlled all river traffic.

Alexander had already selected a crossing point eighteen miles upstream. From his side of the river, it appeared ideal—a heavily wooded spit of land surrounded by a bend in the river. He left the camp at night with a picked force of about fourteen thousand men, including half his Companians, the Guards, three regiments of the phalanx, the Agrianes, and the Scythian horses archers.[2] He left Craterus behind to command the main camp and to cross if he had no opposition once Alexander was across. They took an inland route, and their passage was muffled by a heavy thunderstorm. At the crossing point, skins were stuffed with grass to make floats for individual soldiers, and boats assembled. Alexander was in the first boat as it pushed off at dawn. He had almost reached the other bank when Porus' scouts saw him and rushed off to give the alarm. The landing was successful and unopposed, but Alexander immediately ran into a major problem. The spit of land was actually an island separated from the other bank by a deep but narrow channel. There was no choice but to wade across. Men and horses barely kept their heads out of the water, it was so deep, but they made it. Once across, Alexander put his force in battle order, and marched south, with the horse archers riding in advance.

Porus received the news quickly, and fell into another trap. Across the river, Craterus was giving a good impression of preparing to cross. Porus concluded that the upriver crossing was only a feint and remained where he was. Instead, he sent 2,000 cavalry and 120 chariots commanded by his son. Alexander bloodied this force, killing the prince and sending the survivors reeling back to Porus, who now realized he was facing Alexander in person. Porus marshaled his entire force and moved north to confront the Macedonians and found firm, sandy ground on which to deploy. He stationed his elephants across his front with his infantry behind, cavalry on the flanks, and chariots as a flank guard. Alexander approached and stopped to give his men time to rest. His cavalry deployed on his right, the infantry to the left. He knew the infantry would be decisive in this battle because his cavalry horses feared the elephants and would not approach them.

Alexander's horse archers rode forward to shoot up the left wing chariots that made irresistible targets. Porus sent his left wing cavalry forward to save the chariots, but before they could deploy, Alexander charged them with his Companions. Porus then sent his right wing cavalry to their rescue, riding across the front of his army. As this maneuver began, Alexander detached half his Companions who rode behind their infantry and then crossed in front of them to intercept the moving enemy cavalry. Alexander attacked again. Pressed between two forces, the Indians fell back on their main line and found safety among the elephants. Alexander gave them no respite but had sent his infantry forward. The hedge of sarissas was closing when the elephants and Indian infantry charged. Trained for war, the great beasts trampled through the Macedonian ranks, picking up men and throwing them with their trunks, crushing with their feet. Taking heart, the Indian cavalry attacked the Companions again. The Macedonian infantry held on and fought back savagely. The Companions broke the Indian cavalry and forced it back among the elephants and infantry. Sarissas stabbed at the elephants as arrows and javelins killed their drivers and tormented them. Pain-maddened and without their drivers, the elephants stampeded through their own ranks. The Indian army had become a jumbled mass of men, horses, and elephants ringed by Alexander's cavalry. Every time an elephant tried to escape, a swarm of missiles drove it back into the mass to wreak more havoc. Exhausted and cut to pieces, Porus' army broke and fled through a gap in the surrounding cavalry. The exhausted survivors were intercepted and slaughtered by Craterus who had by then crossed the river.

There remained only one Indian on the battlefield—Porus himself riding in his wooden castle on the back of a great elephant. Single-handedly, he covered the retreat. A tall and powerful man, Porus threw javelins with the force of a catapult, killing and wounding many until the last of his men had quitted the field. At last, wounded and overcome with thirst, he began to back his elephant out of the fight. Alexander was filled with admiration for his conduct and sent messengers to ask for surrender. Porus agreed, and his elephant knelt to let him climb down, and then pulled the javelins from its hide with its trunk.

As Porus approached, Alexander noted his kingly bearing and height, and asked, "What do you wish that I should do with you?"

The Indian replied, "Treat me as a king ought."

Alexander was pleased by the answer and replied, "For my part your request shall be granted. But is there not something you would wish for yourself? Ask it."

"Everything," Porus stated, "is contained in this one request."[3] The dignity of this reply impressed Alexander even more. At last he had found a king worthy to measure honor with. He confirmed Porus in his kingdom and added new territories to it. Porus returned the honors with a steadfast loyalty.

A pall was thrown on Alexander's victory by the death of Bucephalus, who succumbed of wounds suffered in the battle. Of the two cities Alexander founded on the Hydaspes, one was named Nicaea to mark the victory and the other, Buchephalia, to honor his old friend.

Alexander had now heard stories of the rich kingdoms along the Ganges to the east. His enthusiasm grew as he brought his army to the banks of the Hyphasis River (Beas). His Macedonian rank and file, though, had had enough. The monsoon had fallen for seventy days, a depressing experience for European troops who watched everything rot and rust in the constant wet. Love him as they did, they would go no farther. Alexander had not missed the tell-tale signs of a serious morale problem even among his officers. He gathered them and said, "I observe, gentlemen, that when I would lead you on a new venture you no longer follow me with your old spirit." He had called them to decide whether to go on, as he wished, or go back, as they evidently wished. He argued with all of his charm and powers of argument to go on, ending by saying that those who wanted to go were free to do so but that "I will make those who stay the envy of those who return."[4]

This time he was met with stony silence. He begged for an answer repeatedly until the older general, Coenus, stepped forward. He said that he spoke for the common solider, and reminded Alexander of how few Macedonians and Greeks who started out with him at the Hellespont were left. Those few were exhausted morally and physically. They wanted to live long enough to see their families and enjoy the wealth they had earned. "Do not try to lead men who are unwilling to follow you; if their heart is not in it, you will never find the old spirit or the old courage." Return home, he urged, and raise a new army of young, fresh men inspired by the glory and wealth you have showered on your veterans. He ended on a cautionary note, "[B]ut luck remember, is an unpredictable thing, and against what it may bring no man has any defence."[5] The officers applauded; some even wept.

Alexander angrily dismissed them. The next day he brought them back and said he would force no one to go on but was determined to do so himself. "I shall find others who will need no compulsion to follow their King. If you wish to go home, you are at liberty to do so—and you may tell your people there that you deserted your King in the midst of his enemies." Then he shut himself up in his tent and refused to see anyone, sure that a lover's demand would be met. The silence was deafening. He offered sacrifice for favorable omens and received the opposite signs. At last, he gave in and announced that the army would return home. The men surged around his tent, many in tears, and "called down every blessing upon him for allowing them to prevail—the only defeat he had ever suffered."[6] Even his defeats had the seeds of victory. It may have been in these northern campaigns that the young Chandragupta, the first unifier of India, saw Alexander and was inspired by him. Plutarch states that Chandragupta observed that had Alexander pressed on to the Ganges, he would have conquered, so rotten were the kingdoms there.

Alexander would not be entirely bested. He would take the army back by a different route, conquering as they went. This route would be down the Indus to the sea and from there by land along the coast to Iran. His reputation opened many gates, but not all. The nation of the Mallians stood in his way along the lower Hydraotes. Alexander surprised them by coming unexpectedly out of a waterless region, and in a whirlwind campaign he sacked their cities and harried them until the survivors concentrated in their strongest city. His cavalry encircled the city as his artillery drove the defenders from the walls. Alexander broke in through a gate that his Guards had wrenched open and led his men inside, straight for the citadel.

His Guards recoiled from the effort to storm the well-defended citadel walls. There were not enough ladders. Alexander also sensed that the fighting spirit was weak as well. This petty mud fort would not stop him. The men just needed an example, he thought. So seizing a ladder, he threw it on the wall, and scampered up to the parapet and fought off the defenders. His Guards looked up in awe at the warrior king they had always known, standing on the wall in his armor all scarlet and gold, white plumes of his helmet fluttering in the wind.

It lasted for an instant. He was a target for missiles from the neighboring towers, but he would not go back down the ladder. Instead, he jumped down inside the wall where the ground level was higher. His shield bearer, bodyguard, and a sergeant scrambled up after him. Inside the citadel, Alexander had placed his back to the wall as the Mallians came for him. He killed half a dozen with his sword and felled several with stones. The rest drew back to give their archers a chance, just as the three Macedonians came to his aid. The sergeant fell with an arrow in the face and another arrow pierced Alexander through his corselet and into his left lung. His shield bearer threw over him the shield he had taken from the temple of Athena at Troy so long ago. He continued to fight on even though blood frothed with air poured from the wound. An Indian leaped forward to deliver the deathblow, but Alexander cut him down. Finally, he went faint and slumped over his shield.

The Guards outside had been horrified to see the king disappear inside the citadel and frantically tried to find a way in. Some climbed up the mud wall with their fingers; others on the shoulders of their comrades, while others drove stakes into the wall. As each man made it up, he jumped down inside the citadel. Others tore a gate off its hinges and poured through. They overwhelmed the Indians and found Alexander. The cry went up that the king was dead; his men went into a bloody frenzy, killing every living thing in revenge.

Alexander's physician was daunted by the massive nature of the injury and said the huge barbed head would have to be cut out. Alexander calmed him, "What is the moment you are waiting for? If I have to die, why do you not at least free me from this agony as soon as possible? Or are you afraid of being held responsible for my having received an incurable wound?" The physician ordered him to be held tightly as he operated, but Alexander said there was no need and bore the surgery without flinching. Blood gushed from the wound as the arrow was cut out, and he fainted.[7]

The rumor of his death flew to his base camp downriver and threw the army into a panic. They had been stranded at the end of the earth. As soon as he could, Alexander sent them a letter that they refused to believe, calling it a forgery of his officers. Within a week, despite the still-grievous nature of his wound, he was on the move, anxious to dispel the army's fears, traveling south by ship to the army. As the ship approached the crowded shore, the men could only see a motionless Alexander on his pallet. A wail rose that it was his corpse, but he had only to weakly raise his arm, and the sound turned to cheers. More was needed than just showing he was alive. They must see the Alexander they knew—Invincible. He refused a litter, called for a horse, and mounted himself. That act unleashed "a storm of applause so loud that the river-banks and the neighboring glens re-echoed with the noise." He dismounted and walked the rest of the way to his tent, surrounded by men desperate to be near him, to touch his clothes, showering him with blessings, flowers, and wreaths.[8] He had won his lover back.

Because of his convalescence, as well as a Brahmin-inspired resistance, it took him until February (325 B.C.) to finally reach the mouth of the Indus. The religious nature of Brahmin intransigence was entirely new to Alexander, and he responded by hanging every Brahmin he could. That India was the first region to free itself from Macedonian rule after Alexander's death indicates that his successes were merely temporary. At the mouth of the Indus, he ordered the building of a fleet and gave command to his boyhood friend, Nearchus. The fleet was another expression of his yearning for the unknown and would explore the sea route back through the Persian Gulf. He divided the army, giving Craterus the care of Roxane, half the phalanx regiments, the Macedonians whose enlistments had expired, the elephants, and the baggage to return overland by way of Alexandria in Arachosia (Kandahar). The rest of the army would march back along the coast. He was excited by the prospect of besting the exploits of the legendary Queen Semiramis and of Cyrus who had marched armies back the same way and brought out only a few survivors. Despite the romantic appeal of such a route, the journey had been carefully planned. The fleet was intended to carry the supplies of the army, and the army to find water for the fleet.

The march back took the army through the waterless waste of the Gedrosian Desert in September. For the first time, Alexander had seriously miscalculated the logistics requirements and the harsh geography. He had also placed too much reliance on chance. The fleet was delayed by the monsoon and then failed to rendezvous with the army. The pack animals and cavalry horses died or were eaten as the water and supplies ran out. The men abandoned the spoils of India, then their weapons, as they trudged along tormented by the heat. Alexander moved them at night to escape the anvil of the sun, but it was not enough. The irregular water sources were twenty-five to seventy-five miles apart, making any sort of regular march progress impossible. Alexander halted the army several miles from each of these sources to prevent the frantic mob from trampling and fouling the water. The weak were abandoned; there was not transport now to carry them, and they died in their thousands, "poor castaways in the ocean of sand." Of seventeen hundred Companions, barely a thousand survived.

At some point, it was Alexander's will and example that kept the survivors going. He walked at the head of the army, though the pain from his wound should have been staggering. Two scouts returned with a helmet full of water they had scooped from a hollow rock, and presented it in the presence of the halted column. With every man's eyes on the upturned helmet and its obvious contents, Alexander thanked them and poured it into the sand. Arrian wrote as an old soldier of this account. "So extraordinary was the effect of this action that the water wasted by Alexander was as good as a drink for every man in the army."[9]

Chapter 10

"To the Best"

Aʟꜰᴛᴇʀ sɪxᴛʏ ᴅᴀʏs, the survivors staggered out of the desert. Alexander made the first leg of the journey back to Susa a moving party—the men were carried in wagons that were freely supplied with food and wine and wreathed for festival. He had more ominous intentions, however. He had sent messengers on racing camels out of the desert with orders to surrounding satraps to immediately forward supplies to the army. Few had complied. Alexander was finding massive corruption and abuse of power in his absence. A wave of dismissals and executions of both Macedonian and Persian officials followed. Harpalus, his boyhood friend and treasurer, had fled to Greece with 5,000 talents to spend on sedition.

Craterus and the rest of the army joined him in December after a relatively uneventful journey. He was further relieved when Nearchus arrived; Alexander had thought the entire fleet lost. At Susa, he began a serious reorganization of the army that provoked his last serious confrontation with his Macedonians. Historians have argued whether Alexander's "orientalizing" was based on an idealistic attempt to fuse races and civilizations, or whether it was simply an attempt to secure his power base. As with most either/or options, it was probably both. Alexander clearly measured a man's worth by his actions and nobility and had little of the racial attitudes of his Macedonians. On the other hand, he had a huge empire to control, and it was better done with the willing participation of the Persians; Macedonia's population base was a limiting factor. He was also finding the Macedonians increasingly recalcitrant, a marked contrast to the always-obedient Persians.

He fleshed out losses among the Companions by integrating Persian squadrons and even admitted Persians into his Royal Squadron, the *agema*. At this time, the 30,000 Persian youths he had had trained and equipped in the Macedonian fashion arrived. He called them his *epigoni,* or successors. Their enthusiam and the smartness of their drill earned them the scorn of his veterans, who called them "the young wardancers." His most flamboyant device was the marriage of about 100 of his senior Macedonians with high-born Persian wives. At the same ceremony, he married daughters of Darius and his predecessor. So unpopular was this that only one of them would keep his Persian wife after Alexander's death despite the dowries he provided. At the same time, he made a gift to every man who had married an Asian wife and a promise to enlist their sons into the army.

By now the army was in a bad mood, fearing that Alexander intended to replace them, and a further act of generosity was interpreted in that bad light. The fact that he did not detect these feelings says much for his isolation within a more and more elaborate and oriental court and a growing crowd of sycophants. The old Alexander that could warm a frozen soldier by the fire in his own chair had disappeared. He decided to pay off the personal debts of his Macedonians and ordered them to register their obligations. The men jumped to the conclusion that he simply wanted to find the spendthrifts among them, and no one came forward. In his turn, Alexander treated their suspicion as an insult. He ordered the debts paid on the simple presentation of an I.O.U. at the cost of 20,000 talents, an enormous sum. In the spring, he traveled to the Persian Gulf and up the Tigris. At a place called Opis, he called an assembly and announced the discharge of all those Macedonians made unfit by age or impairment. His rewards, he announced, would make them the envy of their kin and an example to fire the young to replace them.

Expecting cheers, Alexander was met with an open mutiny. Cries went up demanding the discharge of the entire army, "adding, in bitter jest, that on his next campaign he could take his father with him—meaning, presumably, the god Ammon." Alexander reacted with fury. He leaped into the mob, arrested thirteen ringleaders, and had them led off to execution. Then he tongue-lashed the stunned crowd: "My countrymen, you are sick for home—so be it! I shall make no attempt to check your longing to return. Go whither you will; I shall not hinder you. But, if go you must, there is one thing I would have you understand—what I have done for you, and in what coin you will have repaid me." He recounted how Philip had raised them from nothing to a great nation, but that was commonplace to what Alexander had done for them. He had laid the world before them, giving freely of all the vast spoil.

> And this I know, that I wake earlier than you—and watch that you may sleep. . . . Does any man among you honestly feel that he has suffered more for me than I have suffered for him? Come now—if you are wounded, strip and show your wounds, and I will show you mine. There is no part of my body but my back which has not a scar; not a weapon a man may grasp or fling the mark of which I do not carry upon me. I have sword-cuts from close fight; arrows have pierced me, missiles from catapults bruised my flesh; again and again I have been struck by stones or clubs—and all for your sakes: for glory and your gain.[1]

He had never failed to honor their dead and reward their families, "for under my leadership not a man among you has ever fallen with his back to the enemy." And now when he wanted to reward the faithful service of those who could no longer serve, they had turned on him. Well, they could all go home and say how they abandoned Alexander to the barbarians, "whom you yourselves had conquered. Such news will indeed assure you of praise upon earth and reward in heaven. Out of my sight!" He jumped to the ground and stormed through the silent mass. For two days, he would see no one, but on the third day he announced the replacement of his senior Macedonians with Persians. He adopted the Persian custom of designating each a royal kinsman who were permitted the ceremonial kiss.

It was a calculated act of manipulation, and it worked. The Macedonians were undone and rushed to his tent, refusing to leave until he had forgiven them. He rushed out, tears in his eyes, but before he could speak, an aged Companion stepped forward to say that they had been wounded that the king had made kinsmen of Persians but no Macedonians. It was a splendid opening, and Alexander made the most it by replying, "Every man of you, I regard as my kinsman, and from now on that is what I shall call you." The old Companion was the first to kiss him, followed by many more. The army marched back to their camp "singing their song of victory at the top of their voices." Alexander exploited the triumph with sacrifices and a great feast for the Macedonians and Persians in thanksgiving for the restoration of harmony, sealing it with prayers that the Macedonians and Persians "might rule together in harmony as an imperial power."[2] After that he released 10,000 men from service and sent them home well paid and with a handsome gift for each man under the care of Craterus.

This event says much of Alexander, but, more important, it says even more of the love affair between Alexander and his army. They were a people warlike by nature and military by training, whose world was little changed from the *Iliad*. Homer put it best:

> One can achieve his fill of good things,
> even of sleep, even of making love . . .
> rapturous song and the beat and sway of dancing
> A man will yearn for his fill of all these joys
> Before his fill of war.[3]

They valued above all else manly virtues that found their greatest expression in war and were the very lethal embodiment of intrepidity, intelligent initiative, and skill.

As the mighty Bucephalus had carried Alexander to the Indus, so had his valiant men supported him, but, as with Bucephalus, there was never any doubt who was master. Alexander had led them on the most rousing adventure of war in all history, filled them with glories and wealth that still dazzle. The animating power of Alexander's genius as leader, general, strategist, logistician, warrior, and hero, rolled into one human being as never before and never since, made them invincible in his hands. And the reverse was true as well. He needed them. Only the Macedonians could give wings to his dreams.

In this mutual need, love was forged, and expressed in the Greek words, to philotimo, literally and inadequately translated as "love of honor," the challenge to be the best, to be greathearted and generous. To philotimo also means the refusal to demean oneself in the eyes of comrades, to be faithful unto death. The soldier whom Alexander pushed out of the ranks for being laggard in his duty suffered a far more damning fate in his own eyes and that of his fellows than any end in battle. He had let Alexander down. Thus the march across Asia was a constant exchange of proofs of love. He would lead and they would follow through every breach and against any vast number that ranged across the field. When he poured the water into the sand in the desert, he gave the purist demonstration of this love. At Opis he was expressing the truth of their relationship when he said he bore no scars on his back and that none of his men had died with their backs to the enemy. Their proof was in the thousands of graves that lined his march of conquest.

In the end, it was the army that could not sustain the love. Alexander asked more of it than even Macedonian flesh, blood, and spirit could sustain. Between Gaugamela and Opis, he had had to again and again breathe life into their love. Then occurred the serious breakdowns in India when the army refused to go on, and at Opis. Their love had also failed when the Guards hung back in storming the Mallian citadel. Alexander, too, had failed. He had sulked one too many times, like Achilles in his tent. At Opis, he said goodbye.

When he let go that love, he let go his anchor. Already, on his return from India he had become more and more autocratic and unapproachable, his court more and more oriental and less healthy for traditional Macedonian frankness. His mood swings became more violent. As he lost touch with his men, he reached for divinity, ordering his oriental subjects to pay him homage as a god. He asked the Greeks to confer that status on him. They did so half amused and half frightened. The death of his devoted friend Hephestion late in the year temporarily unhinged him, leading him to excesses of grief and a funeral that would have bankrupted Greece in its extravagance. He sought relief on a campaign against another Persian hill tribe that thought it could exact tribute from Alexander. He exterminated them as a final death offering for Hephestion.

In the spring he returned to Babylon. The city quickly filled with embassies from Greece and elsewhere as Alexander drew up plans for new conquests in Arabia and cast his eyes westward to Carthage and Italy. One of the ambassadors was Antipater's son, Cassander, come to dissuade the king from retiring his father as regent of Macedonia. Alexander's dislike of the man flared again when Cassander laughed out loud at an old Persian offering his *proskynesis* to the king. Alexander leaped to his feet and beat Cassander's head against the wall.

On the night of the 29th of May, Alexander, already suffering from a slight fever, attended another drinking party and became violently ill. His fever and condition worsened. By late on the 6th of June, he was almost beyond speech and gave his signet ring to Perdiccas in order that business might go on. He knew the end was upon him. Looking at those around his bedside, he whispered, "After my death will you find a king who deserves such men?" They asked him when he wanted divine honors paid him, and he replied, "[W]hen you are happy." As godhead slipped away, the man who had manipulated his lover at Opis faded away, and the human Alexander appeared again.

His troops heard he had died and clamored to see him; "the motive in every heart was a grief and a sort of helpless bewilderment at the thought of losing their king." A second door was broken in his room so that an endless file of men could pass through to see him for the last time. Though he could do no more than struggle to move his head and show with his eyes recognition for each man, that was enough to blow on the embers of memory. Hard men wept as they shuffled through. His officers crowded around to hear his whispered answer to their question of who would succeed him. "To the best," he said. Later in his last words, he foresaw that his friends would hold vast funeral games after his death, anticipating the wars of his successors.[4] On the morning of the 10th of June 323 B.C., he died, just short of his thirty-third birthday.

His friends did indeed hold great funeral games and tore his empire apart in a succession of wars that established their kingdoms. Ptolemy took Egypt and spirited away Alexander's body embalmed in honey to the great new city he had founded on the Mediterranean. Ptolemy built him a marble temple adorned with gold, and his body became the talisman of the city. Alexander's line died at the hands of Cassander who succeeded to the throne of Macedonia. He murdered Roxane and her son Alexander IV, born after his father's death, and Olympias as well. His Macedonian soldiers refused to harm the mother of Alexander, so he turned her over to the families of the men she had murdered. She died like a queen. But Cassander was never free of Alexander. Years later, when he saw a lifelike statue of Alexander at Olympia, he was so overcome that he broke into a trembling sweat.

Almost immediately after his death, rumors that Alexander had been poisoned circulated, and subsequent accounts pointed a finger at Cassander, among others of his officers. Olympias believed it enough later to desecrate the tomb of Ioalus, Cassander's brother and Alexander's cupbearer. The Royal Journal's detailed accounts of Alexander's last days indicate that the cause of death may also have been typhus. The truth will never be known.

His life immediately flew into legend, but the reality was more impressive. Alexander lived his life on his own terms, fixed on a heroic ideal of "warfare and a man at war," and dragged the world in his train. Surely he spoke his own epitaph in India, recovering from the Mallian arrow.

> My own assessment of myself is based on the extent not of my life but of my glory. I could have been content with my father's inheritance, and within Macedonia's bounds have enjoyed a life of ease as I awaited an old age without renown or distinction. . . . But no—I count my victories, not my years and, if I accurately compute fortune's favors to me, my life has been long. . . . Do you think I can relinquish this quest for glory, the one thing to which I have dedicated my entire life? No, I shall not fail in my duty and wherever I fight I shall believe myself to be playing to the theatre of the world."[5]

Notes

Preface

1. Virgil, *The Aeneid*, 1.1, trans. Robert Fitzgerald (New York: Random House, 1983), 3.
2. Carl von Clausewitz, *On War*, 2.2, trans. Michael Howerd and Peter Paret (Princeton, N.J.: Princeton University Press, 1976), 136.
3. J. F. C. Fuller, *The Foundations of the Science of War* (London: Hutchinson, 1926), 98.
4. Robert Jackson, *A Systematic View on the Formation, Discipline, and Economy of Armies* (London: Cadell, 1904), 230.

Chapter 1

1. Plutarch, *Moralia*, vol. III, 179.31, trans. Frank C. Babbit (Cambridge, Mass.: Harvard University Press, Loeb Classical Library, 1931), 53.
2. Plutarch, *Moralia*, 177–79.27, 53.
3. Fontinus, *Strategems*, IV, VII. 35–38, trans. Charles E. Bennett (Cambridge, Mass.: Harvard University Press, Loeb Classical Library, 1925), 325.
4. Alfred S. Bradford, *Philip II of Macedon: A Life from the Ancient Sources* (Westport, Conn.: Praeger), 40.
5. Demosthenes, *Orations,* trans. J. H. Vince (Cambridge, Mass.: Harvard University Press, Loeb Classical Library, 1930), 35.
6. Plutarch, *Moralia,* 177–79.14, 46, 48.
7. Plutarch, *Moralia,* vol. III, 177–79.7; Stobaeus, *Florilegeum,* 3.68, quoted in Bradford, 53.
8. Arrian, *The Campaigns of Alexander,* trans. Aubrey de Selincourt (Hammondsworth: Penguin Books, 1971), 360–61.

9. J. R. Hamilton, *Alexander the Great* (Pittsburgh: University of Pittsburgh Press, 1973), 73.

10. Peter Green, *Alexander of Macedon, 356–323 B.C.* (Berkeley: University of California Press, 1991), 39.

Chapter 2

1. Plutarch, *The Age of Alexander*, 7.2, trans. Ian Scott-Kilvert (London: Penguin Books, 1973), 253.
2. Plutarch, *Age of Alexander*, 7.25, 281.
3. Plutarch, *Age of Alexander*, 7–6, 258–59.
4. Plutarch, *Age of Alexander*, 7–5, 256.
5. Plutarch, *Moralia,* C177–D179.
6. Socrates, quoted in Cicero, *De Officias*, 2.12.43, trans. Walter Miller, cited in Peter G. Tsouras, *The Greenhill Dictionary of Military Quotations* (London: Greenhill Books, 2000), 223.
7. Plutarch, *Age of Alexander*, 259.
8. Plutarch, *Moralia*, 177–179.22, 49.
9. Plutarch, *Age of Alexander*, 7–8, 260.
10. N. G. L. Hammond, *The Genius of Alexander the Great* (Chapel Hill: University of North Carolina Press, 1997), 5–6.

Chapter 3

1. Mary Renault, *The Nature of Alexander* (New York: Pantheon Books, 1975), 12–13.
2. Plutarch, *Moralia,* 180.20, 61.
3. Alfred S. Bradford, *Philip II of Macedon: A Life from the Ancient Sources* (Westport, Conn.: Praeger, 1992), 145.
4. Bradford, 148.
5. Plutarch, *Age of Alexander*, 7.9, 261.
6. Plutarch, *Age of Alexander*, 7.9, 262.

Chapter 4

1. Renault, pp. 62–65.
2. Plutarch, *Age of Alexander*, 7–11, 264.
3. Plutarch, *Age of Alexander*, 7.14, 266.
4. Plutarch, *Age of Alexander*, 7.12, 265.
5. Plutarch, *Age of Alexander*, 7.15, 267.

Chapter 5

1. Diodorus Siculus, *Library of History*, vol. III, 17.17, trans. Bradford Welles (Cambridge, Mass.: Harvard University Press, Loeb Classical Library, 1963), 163. *Spear-won* or *won by the spear* was the Greek equivalent in English of *won by the sword.*

2. Plutarch, *Age of Alexander*, 7.15, 267.

3. James R. Ashley, *The Macedonian Empire: The Era of Warfare under Philip II and Alexander the Great, 359–323 B.C.* (Jefferson, N.C.: McFarland, 1998), 192–95. Numbers in ancient battles are notoriously exaggerated. James Ashley's figures, based on common sense, are used throughout this book.

4. Arrian, 1.13, 79.

5. Aleksander Suvorov, *The Science of Victory*, in *The Greenhill Dictionary of Military Quotations*, ed. Peter G. Tsouras (London: Greenhill Books, 2000), 118.

6. Arrian, 1.17, 76.

7. Curtius, *The History of Alexander* (London: Penguin Books, 1984), 35.

8. Curtius, 35–36.

9. Arrian, 2.12, 122.

10. J. F. C. Fuller, *The Generalship of Alexander the Great* (New Brunswick, N.J.: Rutgers University Press, 1960), 304.

11. Fuller, *Generalship of Alexander the Great*, 305.

12. Plutarch, *Age of Alexander*, 273.

13. Arrian, 2.7, 112.

14. Ashley, 223–25.

15. Arrian, 118.

16. Plutarch, *Age of Alexander*, 275.

17. Plutarch, *Age of Alexander*, 274.

18. Diodorus, 223–224; Curtius, 46.

Chapter 6

1. Arrian, 2.18, 132.

2. Arrian, 2.14–15, 127–28.

3. Curtius, 4.2.1, 54.

4. Plutarch, *Age of Alexander*, 7.30, 287.

5. Curtius, 4..4.10, 60.

6. Diodorus, 17.46, 249.

7. Plutarch, *Moralia*, 180–82.11, 5; Arrian, 2.26, 144.

8. Arrian, 2.26, 144.

9. Arrian, 2.27, 147.

10. Plutarch, *Age of Alexander*, 7.27, 284–85.

11. Homer, *The Iliad* 5.382, 175; Plutarch, *Age of Alexander*, 7.28, 284.

Chapter 7

1. The Macedonian royal emblem was the sunburst.

2. Curtius, 4.7, 80.

3. Arrian, 3.9, 162.

4. Curtius, 4.18–24, 81.

5. Plutarch, *Age of Alexander*, 7.32, 290. Helmets were normally of bronze, and steel was much harder to work, but after his experience at Granicus, it is no wonder he chose it.

6. Described as Indians by the ancient historians, they were from what is now eastern Afghanistan.

7. Ashley, 259–61.

8. Homer, Iliad, 9.2–3., 251.

9. Diodorus, 17.59, 289.

10. Arrian, 3.15, 170–71.

11. Curtius, 5.1.4, 115.

12. Curtius, 5.13.11–14, 116.

Chapter 8

1. Curtius, 5.3.4–16, 122–23.

2. Curtius, 6.6.11, 129.

3. Curtius, 7.5.9, 159.

4. Curtius, 7.5.38, 162.

5. Curtius, 7.7.10–19, 165–66.

6. Arrian, 4.4, 206.

7. Ironically, the Persians did not believe their kings were gods, either, and would have been equally horrified at the thought. Prostration was more an act of submission.

8. Arrian, 4.8, 215.

9. Renault, 155–56.

10. Craterus had commanded the left flank phalanx regiment at Granicus, Issus, and Gaugamela.

11. Green, 367.

12. Curtius, 7.11.7–12, 173–74.

Chapter 9

  1. Ashley, 322.
  2. Ashley, 322.
  3. Arrian, 5.19, 281.
  4. Arrian, 5.27, 295.
  5. Arrian, 5.27–28, 297.
  6. Arrian, 5.29, 298.
  7. Curtius, 9.5.27–28, 224–25.
  8. Arrian, 6.13, 319.
  9. Arrian, 6.26, 339.

Chapter 10

  1. Arrian, 7–10, 363.
  2. Arrian, 7.9–12, 360–67.
  3. Homer, *The Iliad,* 13.743–46, 361–62.
  4. Arrian, 7.27, 394; Curtius, 10.5.5, 245.
  5. Curtius, 9.6.18–19, 226–27.

Bibliographic Note

FOR THE READER who seeks to know more about Alexander, these notes hopefully will provide a useful guide through a very dense thicket.

The vast modern literature on the life of Alexander rests, like an inverted pyramid, on essentially five works of antiquity.

Chronology of sources from antiquity

Diodorus Siculus	Second half, 1st century B.C.
Curtius	Middle 1st century A.D.
Plutarch	Beginning 2d century A.D.
Arrian	Middle, 2d century A.D.
Justin	3d century A.D.

None of these five is contemporary with Alexander, and even the earliest was written three hundred years after his death. These five are based on now-lost contemporary primary and later sources. They often refer to these sources, which, however, remain tantalizingly beyond our reach.

The most reliable of the ancient writers was Arrian (Flavius Arrianus Xenophon) whose *Campaigns of Alexander* (London: Penguin Books, 1971) remains the best of the ancient sources. Arrian was an ethnic Greek but a senior Roman official of the 2d century A.D. An experienced governor and general, Arrian saw Alexander through the practical lens of statecraft and soldiering, which added much to his analysis. He was also, apparently, the most judicious in his use of the primary sources. He weighs the sources carefully and rationally against each other, rejecting the outlandish and the unsupportable. For Arrian, his book on

Alexander was the culmination of a lifelong desire to pay homage to a man who had been a model of conduct and an inspiration. Despite that, his history does not spare criticism where called for.

All five histories apparently made use of the history of Callisthenes, Alexander's official historian, who was executed in India. Arrian, however, additionally based his largely on the histories of Ptolemy, Nearchus, and Aristobolus, all of whom accompanied Alexander on his campaigns. Ptolemy was reputed to be Alexander's half brother and later made himself king of Egypt. His account was a solid military history. Mary Renault, in *The Nature of Alexander* (New York: Pantheon Books, 1975), 38, states clearly that Ptolemy, like all kings, would have been adverse to the public disgrace that would have come from a dishonest account of Alexander when his audience included many who were direct participants in that life. Nearchus was Alexander's boyhood friend and later the highly competent admiral of his fleet. Aristobolus was an engineer whose chronologies and description of the geography and natural world encountered on Alexander's campaigns have been invaluable.

Diodorus Siculus' *Library of History*, books XVI.66–XVII (Cambridge, Mass.: Harvard University Press, 1963), and Curtius' (Qunitus Curtius Rufus) *The History of Alexander* (London: Penguin Books, 1984), and, to a lesser extent, Plutarch's *The Age of Alexander* (London: Penguin Books, 1973), and Justin's *Epitome of the Philippic History of Pompeius Trogus* (Atlanta, Ga.: Scholar's Press, 1994), based their histories, referred to as the Vulgate Tradition, on the history of Cleitarchus who was not a participant in the events he described. According to Waldemar Heckel, in his "Introduction" to Curtius, *ibid.*, 6, Cleitarchus "was prone to exaggerate Alexander's vices, to credit the incredible, to sacrifice historical accuracy for rhetorical effect." The Vulgate Tradition emphasized the heroics of Alexander to contrast them with the vices that eventually overshadowed the heroics. According to N. G. L. Hammond, *Sources for Alexander the Great* (Cambridge: Cambridge University Press, 1993), 21,

Plutarch's account of Alexander's childhood and youth contained in the *Age of Alexander*, on the other hand, appeared to be based on the lost *The Upbringing of Alexander* by Marsyas of Macedon who was brought up with Alexander, probably as a fellow page. Plutarch's objective was not the writing of history but the illustration of character as a guide to later generations.

This struggle between schools resumed in the 19th and 20th centuries in those who pitted the "good Alexander" against the "bad Alexander." W. W. Tarn was the leading exponent of the "good Alexander" school and attributed to him goals of universal brotherhood in *Alexander the Great* (Cambridge: Cambridge University Press, 1948). He has been followed by favorable works, such as Ulrich Wilcken's *Alexander the Great* (New York: W. W. Norton, 1997), J. R. Hamilton's *Alexander the Great* (Pittsburgh, Pa.: University of Pittsburgh Press, 1974) and N. G. L. Hammond's *The Genius of Alexander the Great* (Chapel Hill: University of North Carolina Press, 1997) and *A History of Macedonia* (Oxford: Clarendon Press, 1972). A unique contribution on the literature of Alexander is Mary Renault's book, *ibid.* Like Plutarch, her goal is the examination of character, but unlike Plutarch, she brings a deft use of the historical method. At the same time, she brings the insight into the human psyche that only a great observer of the human condition, a novelist, can bring. She comes down strongly on the side of Arrian. Finally, a key scholar is Eugene N. Borza, whose *Philip II, Alexander the Great and the Macedonian Heritage,* co-edited by W. Lindsay Adams (Washington, D.C.: University Press of America, 1982), *In the Shadow of Olympus: The Emergence of Macedon* (Princeton N.J.: Princeton University Press, 1992), and *Makedonika: Essays by Eugene N. Borza,* ed. by Carol G. Thomas for the Association of Ancient Historians (Claremont, CA: Regina Books, 1995) must be considered.

A harsher view of the Macedonian has been expounded in A. B. Bosworth's *Conquest and Empire* (Cambridge: Cambridge University Press, 1988), Robin Lane Fox's *Alexander the Great* (New York: Dial Press, 1974), and Peter Green's *Alexander of*

Macedon (Berkeley: University of California Press, 1991). In the end, the contending schools still pivot on the same theme as the ancient histories. Those who knew Alexander personally gave the most favorable accounts of the man and the soldier. Perhaps it should rest with that.

As this book is a military biography, the reader should be aware that an important modern addition to the Alexander literature has been a number of military analyses, the first attempt by highly qualified soldiers since Arrian to examine Alexander the soldier. The first of these was the classic *Alexander* by Civil War veteran, Lt. Col. Theodore Ayrault Dodge (New York: Da Capo Press, 1996). Probably the finest of them is Maj. Gen. J. F. C. Fuller's *The Generalship of Alexander the Great* (New Brunswick, N.J.: Rutgers University Press, 1960). Written by one of the finest military minds of the 20th century, this book captures the genius of Alexander as soldier and leader as no other has. James Ashley's *The Macedonian Empire* (Jefferson, N.C.: McFarland, 1998) is an insightful and comprehensive study of not only Alexander's campaigns but the Macedonian art of war. Highly useful in that vein is John Warry and Nick Segunda's *Alexander the Great: His Armies and Campaigns* (London: Osprey, 1998). Perhaps the most specialized military analysis is Donald Engles' masterpiece, *Alexander the Great and the Logistics of the Macedonian Army* (Berkeley: University of California Press, 1978). His detailed examination of Alexander's far-flung campaigns demonstrates that Alexander was one of the finest logisticians of all times, and reaffirms the old adage that "amateurs concentrate on tactics and professionals on logistics."

Index

About the Author

Peter G. Tsouras is currently a senior analyst with the Battelle Memorial Institute in Crystal City, Virginia. For sixteen years previously, he was a military intelligence analyst working for the U.S. Army on the military forces of the Soviet Union and Russia, Iran, and Iraq. His analysis at the operational/strategic level of war was incorporated in the DESERT STORM war plan. As part of a presidential task force, he conducted groundbreaking analysis of Soviet involvement in U.S.–Korean War POW/MIA issues. He served on active duty in the Army in armor, intelligence, and administration, retired as a lieutenant colonel, U.S. Army Reserves, after supporting Civil Affairs operations, and spent time in Somalia. Lieutenant Colonel Tsouras is an accomplished writer of military history and alternate military history, having written or edited twenty-three books, numerous book chapters, and magazine or journal articles. He has had many television and radio interviews and has appeared in television documentaries as a commentator. He is married to the former Patricia Foley and has three children. Pete loves to tell stories in his writing. He remembers the inspiration he received as a child when his Uncle Nick from Sparta set him on his knee, gave him a big silver dollar, and said, "Now let me tell you of Leonidas and the three hundred Spartans."